CONFESSIONS OF A GRIEVER

CONFESSIONS OF A GRIEVER

TURNING A HOT MESS INTO AN HAUTE MESSAGE (LAUGHABLE LESSONS FOR WHEN LIFE JUST SUCKS)

CRYSTAL WEBSTER

NEW DEGREE PRESS

CONFESSIONS OF A GRIEVER

Turning a Hot Mess into an Haute Message (Laughable Lessons for When Life Just Sucks)

ISBN   978-1-64137-486-6 *Paperback*

978-1-64137-487-3 *Kindle Ebook*

978-1-64137-488-0 *Ebook*

To my darling daughter, Madelyn Elizabeth. You made me a mother—no matter what anyone else says. Your very brief life brought me such joy. Because of you I am a better, happier, more compassionate person. Every day in every way I strive to make you proud of me. I look forward to holding you in my arms again—until then, I will hold you in my heart.

CONTENTS

———

LETTER FROM THE AUTHOR

———

FUUUUUUUUUUUUUUUUUUUUUUUUUUUUUUCK!

There. Don't you feel better? Now that we've got that outta the way, we can begin to move forward...

You might like to know that I'm not a swearer, but "Friday" is my *second* favorite F word. Also, I'm not a drinker, but I love a good bottle of vodka; I'm not a gambler, but my favorite-est spot in the whole wide world is Las Vegas; and I'm not a traveler, but I've been around the world a time or two.

If you think this book is gonna be all prim and proper {and bring you to a nice, neat resolution with a pretty little red bow}, I'm sorry, you're mistaken. Close the book, set it down, and back away very slowly...

This book is messy, just like life...just like grief. You'll probably disagree with some of what I have to say, and you might find me crass and ridiculous. That's your prerogative. I do, however, promise you'll be entertained and maybe—just maybe—you'll learn a thing or two along the way. {Did you know that the national animal of Scotland is the unicorn? THERE, you've learned something!}

Every year in mid to late August, there's a day that I just feel "off." I can't focus, I just want to be mad at the world, and eat everything within arm's reach. {Preferably chocolate and potato chips.} It takes me nearly all day before I realize why I'm being a first-class grump: my Facebook feed is full of kids' back-to-school pictures—all the kiddos in their cute little outfits, excited to get back to their friends, with their lunchboxes and backpacks. It always reminds me that my daughter, Madelyn Elizabeth, isn't here on this Earth to experience those firsts.

You see, in May 2010, my husband, Kyle, and I experienced the worst grief we thought to be humanly possible: our Maddie died, just eight hours after she was born, while still in my arms. Her very brief life (and death) shook me to my very core. Even now, over a decade later, I still think about how my life *should* have been.

I *should* be screaming at a ten-year-old to get dressed before her cereal gets soggy. I *should* be {annoyingly} taking pictures with her and the neighbor kids on their way to school. I *should* be irritated the price of markers went up... And, why do I really need thirty-seven boxes of tissues? And why is Target out of glue? And, what happened to last year's backpack? No, we don't need to get a new one every year!

...but I'm not. Instead, I'm sitting in my home office in the fetal position, incessantly scrolling through first day of school pictures unable to look away. As if somehow, magically, Maddie will appear in one of them.

Society believes grief and mourning lasts three, six, or even nine months. {*Maybe* twelve months if it's REALLY bad… you know, like the death of your child.} Then that imaginary buzzer goes off, the button pops and you're all done. (Just like the Thanksgiving turkey) Ta-Daaaaa! You're all healed! Everything is now rainbows and puppy dogs. Time to get over it. Time to move along…

People who haven't truly experienced earth-shattering, mind-numbing grief are under the impression healing is a linear process—you just need to work through the stages. And the harder you try, the faster you will "solve" your grief. {God, how I wish that were true! I'd have a gold medal in "grief healing" if that were actually the case.}

In reality, grief is a topsy-turvy, loop-de-loop of a roller coaster. When you're really in the depths of grief, you feel like you're going to feel this way forever—you don't see a "light" or a "silver lining"—you only see pitch black; and there's no way to "logic" yourself into believing anything else.

Sometimes, the minute you think you're near the finish line, you get transported back to the start. {"Sorry" board game style.} You get pangs of grief at all different times—Alan Wolfelt, PhD calls them "grief bursts." Sometimes you can predict when they'll be triggered—like going to a wedding or a baby shower. But most often, they hit you out of nowhere, upside the head. {Like that random day in August when things just feel off until I realized—halfway through the day—it's the first day of school, and *that's* why I'm a mess.}

While I do believe you can eventually "graduate" from the deep, heavy-on-your-heart, can't-get-out-of-bed, debilitating grief, you'll never actually "get over it." You'll never actually "move on." You will only learn to carry it and move forward toward your *new* normal.

When I was in my "debilitating grief stage" {the five-year period right after Madelyn died when I thought I deserved a plaque just for getting out of bed *and* leaving the house}, I read all the books—and I do mean ALL. THE. BOOKS. About grief, about child loss, and about how to "get normal again." Mostly, I read all those books because they were given to me by people who thought four months was long enough to be sad because of my dead baby.

During that time, I learned there were really only two types of grief books:

1. The research-based, clinical, fact-driven, so-dry-you-wanna-gouge-your-eyeballs-out-with-a-spork books written by a professor with a last name that doesn't have any vowels; or
2. The faith-based, touchy-feely, overly emotional "Jesus did this *for* you not *to* you" books written by a Reverend or Shaman or whoever else can be ordained by an online made-up church.

Both types of books reside in their own special version of La-La Land and forbid you from believing the other type of book even exists {let alone has valid arguments}.

Now don't get me wrong: both these styles of books have bits of information worth reading. But, if you're a "middle of the road-er" like me, you have to sift through a bunch of cr@p to get to the meaty parts. And neither book will just come right out and say what you're thinking—what we're ALL thinking:

"This is the suckiest thing that has ever sucked. How in the hell is the world still spinning when I am in the rock bottom of my suckitude?"

So, I'm here to say it *does* suck! I wouldn't wish this feeling of suck on my worst enemy. **And also** it's nice to know there are others out there who have experienced this amount of suck in their lives too, so you're not all alone in this suckage. I'm here to hold your hand, lend an ear, and sit in the suck with you. In fact, being able to help others know they're not alone – and they're not crazy – is a *huge* part of why I became a grief mentor and how I support others all over the world. {Want some extra support through grief mentoring too? Come check out SharingSolace.com – nudge, nudge, wink, wink.}

Because that's what's missing from the current forms of grief support—the actual SUPPORT.

This book—and the whole concept of Sharing Solace—came out of that suckiness. They are really just tools to bring together a community of "suckers." Where we can be real, honest, and authentic in our experiences. All while making it suck just a little bit less by knowing there are others to walk alongside us on our journey.

──────── Side Note ────────

You'll hear all about Sharing Solace in later stories. The short version? Sharing Solace, launched in 2018, is my way to honor the life, legacy, and love of my Madelyn Elizabeth. It was created to support others as they move along their grief path, no matter what their grief. {Can't wait for more? Flip to page 251 for The Sharing Solace Story}. We help you to Remember. You're not alone.

Contrary to popular belief, grief is not a problem to be solved. It is an ongoing situation that needs to be adapted to and managed. There is no "one answer." There is only "companioning" others along their personal and unique grief journey (another term coined by Dr. Wolfelt).

If you picked up this book, you probably already know grief is all kindsa wonky. {And somehow seems to be able to time travel.} Most grief self-help books tell you to skip around and over parts as you see fit… So, I'm gonna write it that way!! {Plus, if NPH can write a "choose your own experience" book, then so can I!!}

Yup, I'm calling this a "choose your own grief guide." So, read this book cover to cover, or skip around. Or don't! It's totally up to you.

The layout of this book mirrors the path of grief. Your unique grief journey is yours to choose, and so is your interpretation of this book.

So let's start with the first "fork in the road" {just to get this ball rolling}.

If you:

1. Are fulfilled with your book reading experience, all your grief is now completely healed from the above message, and you feel no need to continue reading: please close this book and immediately go to Amazon to leave a 5-star review. {And to purchase at least one copy for all your friends!} …I sincerely hope you can hear the sarcasm in my voice…or:
2. Want to keep reading: do that!

Good! I'm glad you decided to keep reading

{Although I wouldn't really mind that 5-star review at some point. Wink.}

The true goal of these words is to help you to feel not so alone as you walk this path of grief. To help you realize you're not crazy and to give a sense of normalcy to your thoughts and feelings. And...maybe give you some structure, tips, and/or tricks to handle what you're going through—all while having a laugh or two...hopefully... {Fingers crossed!}

You're probably going through a tough time right now: maybe a loved one died; maybe you're getting divorced; maybe you were just diagnosed with an illness; you lost your favorite-est job; or your puppy ran away. Here's the thing: you can grieve (and mourn, which you will learn are completely different) all of these things.

Again, if you're looking for the "standard read" that seems to lay everything out all neat and tidy and wraps it all up with a "happily ever after" as everyone rides off into the sunset, just keep walking {we all know that's not truly how it works anyway; we can't all be Disney princesses}. While you {and me too} would love there to be a twelve-step program, we both understand grief just doesn't work that way. So let's not beat around the bush and fill ourselves with unnecessary and untrue promises and timelines.

You want real-world, not sugar-coated, tried-and-true approaches to navigate your grief (you might not know that's what you want yet, but I promise—it's what you want). These aren't textbook concepts. These are in the trenches, "I threw everything I had against the wall to see what would stick and this is what I got" thoughts.

You're gonna to be spoken to like a real person—four-letter words included, if you haven't figured that out already. Not in theoreticals and hypotheticals. You don't need another professional "should-ing" all over you. You want someone to show you the things that have worked in the past. I'll tell you what worked for me, the stories, the advice, the parables, and the exercises… Hopefully, when you give them a try, they can work for you too.

This is also NOT a book about a higher power controlling your life on your behalf. (Please see my take on that in Take me to Church? on page 89). I believe our lives are partially controlled by the decisions we choose to make and partially by a higher power {call it God, Buddha, Mother Earth, the Universe, little green men—I don't really care what you call it. I like to think it's my Madelyn up there looking out for me as my guardian angel}.

People who haven't experienced the type of loss and grief we have {first, need to knock on wood and thank their lucky stars every single day} don't fully understand how the loss seeps under our skin and into every crevice and area of our life. There is NO getting over it and moving on. Those "non-grievers" treat our ailment like a broken arm: "suck it up," "rub some dirt on it," "walk it off"… They expect our heart to heal like our arm would. They rattle off platitudes as law {like it does anything other than make them sound like an idiot} and give us their answers to questions we didn't ask.

While most people mean well (I really think they do), their words and actions often come across as condescending and patronizing. They make us angrier and more hurt than we were initially, even though their heart is in the right place...

When you hear these words from "outsiders," you start to second guess your process and progress. You begin to feel guilty for your grief {both "guilt" and "grief" are four-letter words in my book}, and you feel lonely. However, trying to isolate yourself from those who "don't get it," and even from those who do, is a recipe for disaster (I promise you).

Hopefully the words on these pages will help you to realize you are NOT CRAZY and this IS NORMAL. Because of your loss, your priorities will shift. You will learn what is truly important in your life, how to set healthier boundaries, and will find yourself becoming a more loving, compassionate, and helpful person {after a brief stint of being the most selfish person on the face of the planet—but, again, it's all part of the healing process}.

Here's one of my favorite quotes {you'll notice, I like to quote quotes}. I often hear it playing on a loop in my head whenever I need the reminder:

You either get bitter or you get better. It's that simple. You either take what has been dealt to you and allow it to make you a better person, or you allow it to tear you down. The choice does not belong to fate, it belongs to you.

—JOSH SHIPP

Here's to becoming a better, not bitter, person. Are you ready?

WHY I'M THE ONE WRITING THIS (AND WHY IT NEEDS TO BE WRITTEN)

Most of the books I've read on grief, loss, and mourning are written by clinical therapists or researchers... Or therapists turned researchers, or researchers turned therapists... Sometimes, they had a traumatic childhood, which led them down the path of grief work. Sometimes they were already a practicing therapist and something tragic happened that changed their career course. Either way, they've been trained in physiotherapy, so while their writing is still very interesting, it is often filled with the scientific "mumbo-jumbo" I just don't understand. Words like "cognitive dissonance," "super ego," "reaction formation," and "schema."

Those same experts also have a preconceived notion of what they should expect (and what society expects) throughout the "grieving period" because of that schooling. I've got none of that and had no idea what I was doing or what to expect. I was just "feeling my feels" and "thinking my thoughts."

While I've read/watched/listened to just about everything by the likes of Dr. Alan Wolfelt, Brené Brown, Megan Devine, Elisabeth Kübler-Ross, and others (and will even reference them along the way), I didn't actually do the research, nor am I trained to decipher it. That's not my jam {I can't even play the instrument}. I'll leave that to others who know what they're doing.

Other than thinking psychology was mildly interesting in college, the way the mind works isn't via "facts and figures," so my accounting brain just couldn't fully comprehend... So, for years, I went back to the "real world"—to number crunching in corporate America.

Then, in 2010, I was pregnant; just trying to live my life. My daughter, Madelyn Elizabeth, died (I promise, you'll hear the whole story later), and I found I was swimming {ok, more like drowning} in my own self-deprecating thoughts. I didn't know what to do...and when you don't know what to do, you go back to the basics: I started watching self-help YouTube videos, reading books...pretty much doing whatever I could to get out of my own head {or at least try to figure out what the hell was going on in there.}

So, THAT'S where my learnin' comes from: the school of hard knocks. I'm "grief smart," not "book smart." Book smart is great and all (and I did get a lot of that from the experts), but you gotta have equal parts of both to make it in this wild, wild west of mourning.

Going into this, I didn't have any preconceived notions of what was "supposed" to happen or a time frame for it. I was {still am and will always be} voyaging through my grief. In a lot of ways, I have taught myself to put on a mask in public and "fake it till you make it," but eventually, that mask begins to wear thin.

While my story is the loss of a child and the dream of having a biological family, I truly believe that grief is grief, and loss is loss. Loss does not always equal death. It could be the loss of a relationship, a job, a dream, a diagnosis...the list goes on. But I hope you won't shut out the ideas in this book because my story doesn't line up perfectly with yours. If we allow ourselves to seek out and find the similarities in each other's grief stories {instead of fighting to keep our story uniquely the "best"}, we can all work toward fixing our broken hearts that much sooner and find our new happy just a little more easily. The sooner we are able to do that, the sooner we're able to help others do the same.

If you look solely at the numbers, my story is not all that unique. One in four women suffer a pregnancy or infant loss in their lifetime. One in eight couples suffer from infertility (*and*, according to the National Survey of Family Growth, a million couples suffer secondary infertility). *Also*, every death (expected or otherwise) substantially affects six adults... that's a whole lot of people picking up what I'm putting down.

Regardless of these statistics, for years I wouldn't even acknowledge that others could fathom the deep pit of grief I was in. Talk about absurd! Twenty-five percent of ALL WOMEN IN THE WORLD have lost a child. My story can be both uniquely mine *and* have commonalities with others. That said, it's still my grief to grieve.

It took me way too long to find my "new happy"—almost eight years. And, don't get me wrong, sometimes I still lose it and have to go looking again. If I can help you move toward finding your "new normal" {either through the words on these pages, grief mentoring, our beautiful products, and/or The Feel Your $&*@# Feel Experience} sooner than you would have otherwise, I feel like I've done my job.

So come on in and stay a while. Grab a cup of your favorite beverage {...vodka?...} and let's learn from each other's experiences. I might not be the most eloquent in what I have to say, or the smartest at saying it, but I'd like to think I might just have a few things worth sayin'.

HOW TO USE THIS BOOK

———

Warning I'm about to make a wildly inappropriate comparison here. Are you ready?

Use this book like you would the Bible.

Now, before you smite me, let me explain.

First, I do not believe the words on these pages compare to those of the Bible, Koran, or the Torah. {If you're going to accuse me of blasphemy, at least let me come up with a better, more offensive reason…like when I do end up going to jail for stealing, it's gonna be because I held up a bank for a billion bucks, not because I walked off with some gum from the 7-Eleven. I'm going down in a blaze of glory!}

What I DO mean is that (just like the Bible) I doubt you will pick up this book and read it cover to cover, A to Z (or FUUUUUUUU to the last period in this book's case.) This work has been specifically and strategically arranged in the order it's in. The chapters are "Dan Brown" short by design. You're INTENDED to skip from the front to the back and around again.

I suspect you will read a story or two then put the book down, leave it on your nightstand for a week, scribble in the margins, highlight passages that speak to you, forget where you left it, dog-ear your favorite story, give it to a friend to borrow, six months later remember who you lent it to and ask for it back... If this book is half as "destroyed" as my blue Precious Moments Bible I got for my First Communion by the time you're done, then (again) I've done my job.

There are a few {very symbolic} reasons the book is written and laid out the way it is:

- If you chose to read this because you yourself are going through a traumatic loss, your "grief brain" is at an all-time high. If you've never experienced "grief brain" {lucky ducky!}, it's like having ADHD without medication while being highly sleep deprived. {Plus, there's a toddler in the other room while you're trying to do pretty much anything else.} You just can't focus on anything for more than about 3.4 minutes at a time. {If you happen to be one of the select few, like me, who had "grief brain" on top of "pregnancy brain"... I'm sorry, you're just screwed for a while. Be gentle with yourself.}
- Everyone's grief journey looks different: some prefer to "dig a hole," while others just want to "climb a tree." Neither is right or wrong. Each person has the opportunity to "choose their own grief adventure." For a while, you will swell with the waves and go where the tide takes you. But eventually, you will begin to make decisions that, little by little, will guide you along your unbeaten path. You may move forward, backward, or side to side. You have to find

your own way toward your own "new normal"—and you may have to make a few U-turns in the process.

- Grief is not linear: So why should a book about grief be written linearly? I've said it before and you know I'll say it again: grief doesn't just ebb and flow—it also time travels, shape shifts, throws tantrums like "sugared up" tiny humans, and jacks with the space-time continuum. You're *intended* to flip around in this book: front to back and back to front. This book is written to mirror how I've felt the last decade—and how you probably feel too.

Technically, I guess you *can* read this book cover to cover—if you really wanted to. Honestly, it will make about as much sense as grief does. However, I wouldn't recommend it. If you do choose to read this linearly, you will miss out on the symbolism. The road of grief is a never-ending game of Sorry!® {this sentence brought to you by Hasbro}: just about the time you think you're about to "win," some jerk comes along and sends you back to the start. {In this case, "that jerk" being your d@mned, dirty emotions and triggers.}

You will see there are seven sections in this book representing the seven stages of grief: shock, denial, anger, bargaining, depression, testing, and acceptance (more on those stages next). I have broken up my personal story, research, anecdotes, and tips and tricks {loosely} into these seven sections. If you choose to read from cover to cover, you will read about each section in the order Dr. Elisabeth Kübler-Ross initially wrote them.

– OR –

You can begin by reading my personal story, from 2009 through today {I start each section with my personal experience with each "stage" of grief}, then circle back around to the research and tidbits within each section. If you choose to read this way, you will probably see me as some crazy person with ego issues and a God complex. {See above.} Obviously, I don't recommend you reading it this way either. {I want you to like me.}

– OR –

{And this is the option *I* prefer!!}

Read it as the stories intrigue you and feed your soul. At the end of each story, you will be given a choice as to how you would like to proceed. Maybe you wanna know why a story is titled as such. Maybe one sounds less crap-tastic than the others. Maybe you don't particularly care for any of them, so you just randomly flip the page.

This option, to me, more closely resembles how my personal grief journey has worked. I *think* I'm continuing down the "right" path of healing only to come to a fork in the road and decide to turn back around {or teleport back to the beginning altogether}.

This book is written with no real "end point" in mind as you never truly "get over" or "end" devastating grief. You move beyond the "devastating" part, but the "grief" part always lingers. You learn to carry it with you in a way that makes it tolerable. That said, you *will* find you arrive at a kind of homeostasis, where you are able to see both the forest AND the trees of your life and maybe even see a little light between the branches.

STAGES OF GRIEF

Before we get into this too deeply, let's get some of the book learnin' out of the way {you knew it was gonna happen}:

We've all heard about the "stages" of grief. In fact, if you're like me, you've probably had those stages used against you along your grief journey because you're not "far enough along" or "seem to be backtracking."

In case you are unfamiliar, the stages of grief are:

- Shock*
- Denial
- Anger
- Bargaining
- Depression
- Testing*
- Acceptance

*These two are not in the initial Stages of Grief by Elisabeth Kübler-Ross, MD, but she later refined her model to include Shock and Testing to help "smooth out" the process, show transition, and facilitate change.

Here's what grief (according to the above stages) is "supposed" to look like:

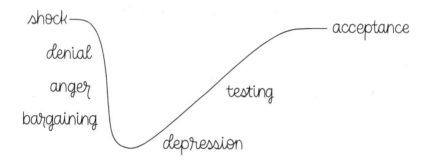

And here's how I feel my grief experience has looked thus far:

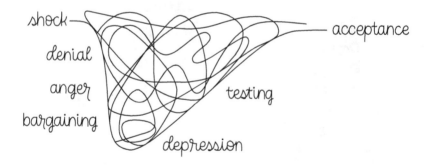

You can probably figure out what each stage consists of just by reading the title, without much further definition. But I'll give you some more context anyway—because I can:

Shock—That initial paralysis. You can't even comprehend what's happening or digest the information. Your brain and body "shut down" and basically stop taking in new information.

Denial —You begin to comprehend, but don't really believe it. You're overwhelmed. You're just trying to get from one minute to the next. Blocking out all feelings is your coping mechanism. {Walking Zombie Pt. I.}

Anger—You're just mad. How can bad things happen to good people? You might get mad at the situation, the people, the world, and even God. You push everything and everyone away. Your anger knows no bounds and you might {ok, probably *will*} find yourself angry at people/things not even attached to the specific situation.

Bargaining—It's time for the "if onlys" and "what ifs." You hope you'll wake up and this was all just a bad dream. You try to rewind the clock to "play it out differently." {Guilt and Bargaining are BFFs—they tend to go everywhere together.}

Depression—Everything reminds you of what happened and what you don't have now. Everything. You think you'll feel this way forever and there is no reason to do anything anymore {get out of bed, eat, function, you name it}. Life has no meaning. You're in a fog of sadness and wonder. {Walking Zombie Pt. II.}

Testing—Once you've hit your personal "rock bottom," you begin to move, ever so slowly, out of your depression comfort zone to see if there is any semblance of a life left "out there" for you to live.

Acceptance—You are not "all better"...but you're finding ways to move forward toward your "new happy." You learn to carry your grief and sorrow with you daily and find ways to receive pleasure in your new normal. You cannot replace what you have lost, but you can use your loss to evolve into a "better" version of yourself. Finding acceptance does not mean you will never "relapse" back into a previous stage of grief. But, you will just find you spend more and more time in the acceptance stage as time go on.

Now, here's the thing about the Kübler-Ross study that was presented in 1969 and the stages of the study: the book Dr. Kübler-Ross wrote titled *On Death and Dying*[1] is just that, a book and study following those who had to come to terms with **their** ultimate death. She interviewed patients with terminal illnesses and discussed how their impending end affected them as a person. Here, let me say that another way:

THE RESEARCH SAYS THESE STAGES ARE ABOUT PEOPLE WHO ARE ABOUT TO DIE, NOT FOR THE PEOPLE THAT ARE GRIEVING AFTER THAT PERSON'S DEATH.

Why is this an important distinction? Because you can't get mad at a penguin for not flying. You can't compare apples and tomatoes for not growing and tasting the same. You

---

[1] Kübler-Ross, MD, Elisabeth. *On Death & Dying: What the Dying Have to Teach Doctors, Nurses, Clergy, and Their Own Families.* Scribner, 1969.

can't use a rule book for a different game and be mad your opponent is "playing wrong."

Here's another thing about the study. Urban legend has it that one of Dr. Kübler-Ross's regrets is that she called the categories "stages." She did later say that "she never conceived of the stages as linear or all-encompassing."

Using the term "stages" implies that you finish one before moving on to the next {and you are unable to backtrack to an earlier stage, similar to an old-school Mario Brothers Nintendo game}. This is false in so many, Many, *MANY* ways; unfortunately, the only way to truly know is by going through this deep personal grief yourself.

Kübler-Ross did, much later, go back and tie these stages to any type of grief (death of a loved one, end of a relationship, job loss, etc.), similar to how I elaborated above. The problem is it's not as clean of a fit. There are more caveats, more sub-stages, more nuances…

So what does this mean to you?

It means you gotta play "The Game of Grief" like you do when you're playing canasta with Grandma Rosemary. You THINK you know all the rules of the game, but don't be surprised when Gammy Rose "remembers" that you can only play the eight of clubs when a one-eyed Jack is showing.

You're allowed to move forward with the new rules, or you can throw a hissy fit and "angry man" style flip the table—dice, meeples, cards, pawns, and box included—and start all over again. {Yes, I am well aware I compiled about forty-seven different games into this metaphor...that's how forked up grief can be.}

This model is just that: A MODEL.

It's a proposed structure, a suggestion, a general road map. There is no right way to get from point A to point B. The goal is to just move toward point B. You need to move at your own pace: backtrack/sidetrack/forward-track however it feels right to you. Remember: your grief is a loop-de-loop of a choose your own experience.

Don't judge yourself based on these stages {they don't fully apply to you anyway}. And don't even think of these as stages! Think of them as route markers of where you could possibly be along your journey. And know that you might need to circle back around to get your bearings before working your way forward again.

Because your grief journey, much like mine, will have many twists and turns and forks in the road, I want to remind you this book is designed as a "game-book," a "Choose Your Own Grief Guide," if you will. Just like life, and The Game of Life {this sentence also brought to you by Hasbro}, you will have the opportunity to take any number of paths.

Do you take the path less traveled? CHOOSE the journey that will make you better.

SHOCK - MY PERSONAL STORY

———

Once upon a time in a land far, faaar away… {Isn't that how all "good" stories start?}

It was Halloween 2009. I woke up my husband, Kyle, way too early that morning. I had something important to tell him. He was gonna have to "dress up" for Halloween—in sandals with socks, a bucket hat, and maybe even a fanny pack. He was going to be a daddy. We were pregnant with our first child.

Less than one week later I woke up way too early for another, far more nefarious reason. An incessant ring on my cell phone from an unknown number. Again, and again. Ring, ring, ring. I'd just gotten a new phone and didn't have all my numbers programmed in it {this was 2009, I mean, I still had a flip phone}. It was my dad on the other end from a business conference. My dad never calls me—or travels.

"Kent and Jane died. Get over to Mom's right now. She doesn't know yet and you need to be there to tell her." Still groggy, epic bedhead, and probably the worst morning breath ever, I shake Kyle awake and we zoom across town. I'm not even sure I let him slow down before I jumped out of the car.

My mother is sitting on the front porch steps. Cell phone in one hand, dog leash in the other. She was taking our family puppy for a morning walk when her cousin called to "see how she was doing with the news."

Her cousin didn't know she had BROKEN the news.

Kent, my mother's brother (eleven years her senior) and Jane, his wife (more like my mother's sister than an "in-law") were tragically killed late the night before on their way home from a Nebraska Cornhusker football game (BGR!). It was a series of unfortunate events, plus an inattentive eighteen-wheel truck driver.

"Luckily," the coroner said, they were killed on impact, didn't suffer, and probably didn't even really know what was happening.

Although Kent and Jane lived halfway across the country on the tundras of Alaska most of the year, and I rarely had the opportunity to see them, they held a very special place in my heart. They, in my opinion, were the epitome of saints on Earth. Neither of them had a very easy life—physical concerns, emotional issues, addictions. I still, to this very day, have never seen anyone turn a lifetime of pain and setbacks into such purpose. They were the most loving, friendly, inspiring humans. To know them was to love them.

The funeral preparations and events that followed were a complete blur. I remember being physically sick and lethargic from pregnancy hormones but having the luxury of "playing them off" as *just* immense sadness {looking back, I know it was actually very much both}. I was walking through a thick, dense fog while feeling completely wrapped in love. To this day, I still have never seen a service so well attended with so many loving friends and family.

I struggled after the funeral, though I rationalized my "funk" with a multitude of reasons and excuses:

- I'd just moved back to my hometown after being away for two years {culture shock is a real thing even when moving back home}.
- I was living with my in-laws in the 10 ft. x 10 ft. bedroom my husband grew up in.
- I was pregnant and doing my best to hide it from half the people I was living with.
- I was starting a new job, and a new career, as a business owner {and I had no idea what I was doing}.
- I was trying to find the "perfect house" to move my "perfect soon-to-be family" of three into {with an engineer-ish husband who had very specific and non-negotiable criteria}.

It was a few months after Kent and Jane's funeral, and I thought life was back to "normal" when I overheard someone asking my husband, "What happened to the Crystal we know and love?"

Luckily, the next day I had a scheduled doctor's appointment. I think I had subconsciously known something wasn't right for a while, so I convinced my doctor to prescribe me antidepressants {you know, the really gooooood ones}. While I understood the research, many medications were not encouraged to be taken during pregnancy, and the studies on mothers' depression were not too promising either. I took the lesser of the two evils.

Even medicated, the holidays were hard that year. {And every year after that, let's be honest.} Thanksgiving was takeout food through tears. For Christmas, the family went through the motions...because that's what you do during the holidays—you do family holiday things. Yes, the immediate family was excited to welcome the first grandbaby into the family, but that anticipation was overpowered by the sorrow of what was missing. Baby Webster wasn't quite "real" yet, and Kent and Jane's death very much was.

The next few months were not particularly eventful {thank you, baby Jesus}. My belly grew and we bought a new house to bring our little one home to. I was one of those moms that didn't want to know the sex of the baby until it arrived. Others would ask the question, and I would give our standard response: "as long as it's happy and healthy that's all that really matters."

...little did I know...

During what we thought was a routine ultrasound at thirty-two weeks, we heard the words no parents should ever have to hear:

"Something doesn't look quite right. I'm going to speak with the doctor."

The technician could have been gone five minutes or five years. Time completely stopped for me. When she returned she told us she was not allowed to give us any further information, only a doctor could do that, and we were instructed to go immediately to my general practitioner's office, across town. Something had to be wrong; it was already well after five p.m.

Clearly, the office staff was waiting for us. We were immediately ushered back to a patient room, and within moments our doctor appeared with red, puffy eyes. "We don't know exactly what's going on, but this is not good. I've scheduled you to meet with the high-risk OB tomorrow morning, and we should know more after that appointment. Go home, get some sleep, and we'll get more information tomorrow."

...Yeah, uh-huh. Okay. I'll just go home, make some dinner, watch some reality TV, and hit the sack early. Well, truthfully, that's exactly what I did. I went home, pushed some leftover takeout around my plate until it was cold, stared at a TV with rabbit ears, "watching" the only channel we could get reception for, and then climbed into bed early, exhausted from the events of the day.

Only, there was no sleeping. There was no relaxing. My body was numb from the information overload, and I couldn't really understand what had happened anyway. What was going on? What did all this mean? While I was scared out of my mind, I assumed {and hoped} this appointment with the specialist would go like every other specialist appointment I'd ever had. The general practitioner sees something weird but doesn't know enough, so they send you over to a specialist, only to have them tell you everything is fine.

That's what's gonna happen tomorrow, I just know it.

Now it's your turn. You decide how you'd like to move forward:

Want to know what really *did* happen? (Umm, duh, you're not an idiot and you've read the cover of this book.) Turn to **page 65** for **Denial—My Personal Story**.

Don't believe I should have the right to be sad…just yet? I disagree; let's argue about it. **Turn the page** for **Any Loss is Grieveable**.

Do you think this book is all kinds of weird and you're not sure you're interested in reading the rest? {I mean really, who compares their book to the Bible!?!?!—even if it does make perfect sense.} Turn to **page 83** for **This Might Not Be Your Time**.

ANY LOSS IS GRIEVEABLE

According to the Merriam-Webster Dictionary {no relation}, the definition of grieve is "to cause great distress."

To take it one step further, distress is defined as a painful situation; pain or suffering affecting the body, a bodily part, or the mind.

Nowhere in any of the above definitions does it say anything about death. Yeah, your mind immediately goes to "dead" when you hear the word "grief" {that's the easy answer, the low-hanging fruit}.

But, grief can come in many forms:

- the death of a person {duh}
- loss or end of a relationship
- death or loss of a pet
- loss of a job
- loss or change in a situation or circumstance
- loss of a dream or expected outcome
- loss of personal possessions
- change in your physical or emotional environment
- diagnosis or (chronic) illness
- stubbed toe

- discovering unicorns are not real {and that you cannot have one for your birthday...}

No, really. While this is not an all-encompassing list, compare each of these bulleted items with the definitions above. You can grieve each and every one of those scenarios to varying degrees {and if you EVEN try to tell me you can/can't grieve some of those—or how "hard" you should grieve each of them—please see Don't You Call My Husband an @$$hole on page 117 before I punch you in your throat}.

Now, let me tell you a ridiculous story about how you can grieve just about anything {inanimate objects included} and how grief is all relative to your present situation and mental state:

In high school and college I drove a blue 1988 Toyota 4Runner. My parents bought it used, and it probably had 100,000 miles on it by the time it was mine to drive. But ohhhh, that car was sweet! Girls wanted to be me, and boys wanted to be with me. It had a moon roof, a tailgate window that retracted by putting the key in the lock, and a rag top for the summer, which when folded down basically gave you a convertible pickup. It even had a personalized license plate—"SLEEPR."{Because my dad works in the O.R. as a nurse anesthetist, not because I slept around. Looking back on it, maybe not the best idea for a teenage girl's car.}

I didn't take the best care of that car. There was always homework, textbooks, clothes, leftover fast food, CDs {remember those?!?}, you name it, in the back seat {again, I was a teenage girl}, but dang did I love that car more than life itself!

One evening, a couple of years into college, I got a call from my mom on my "Zack Morris" cellphone during *Gilmore Girls*. {The car at this point is well over a dozen years old... don't do the math. I'm twenty-three today—that's my story and I'm sticking to it!}

"Your dad and I don't think you should be driving the 4Runner to school anymore. It's starting to have problems and school is just too far away. Next time you come home, we'll have you swap out for another car."

"...What?!?"

"Yeah, it's just not safe anymore for you to drive the couple hours to and from school. The regulator is going out, the starter is about to need to be replaced..."

"...What?!?"

"Next time you're home..."

"I can't talk to you right now."

I hung up the phone and had to take slow, deep breaths to calm down. I cried myself to sleep that night, knowing my time with my beloved 4Runner was nearing the end. I was devastated.

———————————— Flash Forward to 2011 ————————————

Madelyn's physical presence had already come and gone from my life. I was out with a group of friends for a much needed evening of relaxing. My first ever, brand new, completely paid off blue Toyota Prius {I have a thing for Toyotas and the color blue} was in the parking lot waiting for me.

After a couple adult beverages, too much fried food, and so much laughter I could barely breathe, I walked out the door to head home.

There was my car, just where I had left it. And there was my rear bumper, ten feet away, NOT where I had left it.

"Well, that sucks."

After a big ol' sigh and a heavy shrug, I picked up the bumper and shoved it into my trunk, and I went on my way home. I continued to drive without a rear bumper for months before I decided it was probably time to have it reattached.

Maybe at that point in my life I was in a better financial situation: "If money can fix it, then it's not really a problem." But, more likely, my Maddie had very abruptly put things into perspective for me.

Now, I fully understand things can be replaced and repaired. But, come on, the entire rear bumper of my brand new car?! THAT was a BIG "thing!"

In all honesty, if Madelyn hadn't come and gone from this Earth to teach me this lesson—just one more time—I can all but guarantee I would have flipped out right in the middle of the parking lot. I would have made a huge, obnoxious scene, letting it ruin my {and probably everyone else's} entire night. Completely negating the merriment just moments earlier.

The lesson of relative grief is one of those lessons that needs to be learned over and over (and over) again, and I believe you can't truly "learn" it until you lose something you can never replace.

<hr/>

Side Note

This story is not to be confused with the "You can milk anything with nipples" scene from *Meet the Parents,* which I think about every single time I read this. {I don't know why I originally thought of that scene when writing this, but now, once you get it, you will never *not* think about it either. "I have nipples, Greg. Could you milk me?"}

<hr/>

Now it's your turn. You decide where to go next:

Still don't believe you have the right to grieve any of the list above? Sounds like you need some permission to have real, live, human feelings. **Turn the page** for **Permission.**

Like pop culture references and ridiculous stories? How about another one? Turn to **page 193** for **Two Truths {and a Lie}.**

Think this story about my two blue Toyotas is absurd? {PS: it is absurd, but it makes a point.} Let's talk about some other absurd things. Turn to **page 135** for **You Will Second-Guess.**

PERMISSION

::Clearing my throat:: **Hear ye, hear ye,**

I do hereby and henceforth grant you permission to be *human*. However, I want to remind you, you do not need anyone's approval to grieve and have real, raw emotions.

That being said, if you're anything like me, you think you can't always take time for yourself without the A-OK from someone else. If that's you, here it is:

PERMISSION SLIP

I grant permission to _____
NAME
for the purpose of _____
_____

_____ for the duration of _____
MIN/HRS/DAYS

You are allowed to {check all that apply}

☐ cry   ☐ have a pity party
☐ scream   ☐ break/throw things
☐ sleep   ☐ not shower or bathe
☐ veg out   ☐ stay in bed all day
☐ be selfish   ☐ eat/drink what you like

Crystal
_____
Grantor's Signature

Be you. Have emotions. Throw things. Yell and scream. Cry. Be mad. Be angry. Be inconsolable. Bake. Write. Hike. Read. Run. Think the dark thoughts. Speak the happy musings. Go down the rabbit hole. Ask "what if?" Say "should have." You are allowed to do what you need to do to process the circumstances you've been through. No one can tell you the right way to do that.

Self-care is not self*ish* and is often a form of self-preservation. You need to allow yourself the opportunity to safeguard your well-being. One of my favorite sayings is "You can't pour from an empty cup. Take care of yourself first." As a woman {I can't speak for the men}, I often feel it's my job to care for friends and family. It's nearly impossible to care for others if you don't take care of yourself first. You just won't have the energy and wherewithal.

Now, let's also talk about self-compassion. Yup, self-CARE and self-COMPASSION are different. Self-care is the physical act of doing things to increase or maintain your health and welfare. Self-compassion is having sympathy and concern for yourself when you are suffering.

Can we all just try to remember there's only one Mary Poppins—practically perfect in every way? Her name is Julie Andrews {I will also accept Emily Blunt—if I have to...}. We *try* to "be all" and "do all"–all by ourselves—and deep down (I hope) you know we just "can't even."

Allowing yourself, especially when you're grieving, to NOT be everything to everyone is my version of **self-compassion**. Understanding, allowing, and not beating yourself up because things "fall through the cracks," or you forget about something, or you just can't bring yourself to do something that is self-compassion.

Again, you are human. Sh!t happens, time gets away from you, you can't get yourself out of bed. It's okay. Let yourself skip out on the non-mission critical things for the time being. Say "No, I can't" when asked to do something, if you know it will drain you—and stop there. No explanation necessary! "No" is a complete sentence.

Self-care is a little bit easier to understand. We've ALL heard of self-care. It's enjoying a long cup of coffee, a hot bubble bath, or a good book. It's getting a massage, or your nails done. It's a little retail therapy. It's talking to a friend on the phone about nothing. It's playing Candy Crush on your tablet. It doesn't have to be expensive or time-consuming.

One of my favorite things to do is sit in the car in the rain—hearing the water hit the windows {and not getting soaked} while being close-ish to nature. For me this is so soothing. Sometimes I'll read a book, or listen to the radio, or just sit in silence. {My alternative, if it's not raining, is to go to the drive-through car wash and crank the tunes.}

This stuff is so very important that I wanna bullet point it, just one more time, for you:

- You have my permission to feel your feels and grieve how you need. Give **yourself** the same permission.
- Self-compassion and self-care are not self*fish*; it is self-*preservation.*

- It's essential you allow yourself the space for self-compassion and self-care.
- YOU ARE NOT BEING SELFISH WHEN YOU ARE CARING ABOUT YOUR OWN WELL-BEING.

Now it's your turn. Where do you wanna go next?

Wanna know more about self-care and maybe some ideas of ways for you to take care of you? Turn to **page 147** to **Do More Good Sh!t**.

Now that you have your own permission slip to be human when grieving, let's talk a little more about the right way to do it. **Turn the page** for **There Is No Right Way to Grieve**.

Think you're being set up to fail? Or, it's all just some cosmic lesson to learn? Sometimes you just need to remember **This Is Not a Test**. Turn to **page 201**.

THERE IS NO RIGHT
WAY TO GRIEVE

If I've learned anything along this wild ride, it's that no one grieves in exactly the same way, and everyone needs to do it at their own pace and on their own terms.

I'm a "lay on the sofa, yes, I'm watching that static on the TV, put all the food in my mouth, don't even *think* about asking me to move" griever. My hubby is a "rewire the house, clean out the basement, smash a hole in the dining room wall with a hammer to see what's behind it, move the washer and dryer, rebuild a hot-rod" griever. It took a little bit to realize that we were both grieving properly, just in different ways. It was backward from what the other expected, but that didn't make it wrong.

I know others that are "give up all forms of' 'adulting,' only eating cereal and Pop Tarts, start throwing axes, stay up all night, and turn the music up to eleven" grievers. {Let's be honest, that's a little bit me too.}

You might be a "this house has to be spotless" griever, or an "I just wanna be mad and throw things" griever, or an "I'm leaving town" griever, or a "let's go buy some expensive, completely unnecessary sh!t" griever, or even a "screw it, I ain't doin' nothing" griever.

You read these books on grief, and they all say about the same things: "I was sad, I didn't wanna get outta bed…" But, here's the thing; that's not always the case. Sometimes moving and being active is your version of "not getting out of bed." Not only that, those books forget to tell you how they went from "I don't wanna get outta bed" to "I'm a fully functioning member of society again." {Or they don't tell you because they don't actually know how it happened.}

I think everyone going through something this traumatic has to hit rock bottom before they can start on their way back up again. You gotta get to your own personal version of "there's only one way left to go and that's up." But, it's different for each person, and under each circumstance. You just kinda *know* when you've gotten to your rock bottom {if you haven't yet, I promise you will, and you'll know you're there}. Then, you have two options:

- You can either live here in the bottom of the pit you dug for yourself or
- You can actually start your way back up

But, again, the books forget to tell you how: how to actually start climbing back up again. Part of that is because it's different for everyone. Every type of "griever" has a different way to start that climb.

For me, it was baby steps: I didn't quit grief "cold turkey." {If that's even possible.} I didn't jump out of bed one day and run a marathon. I didn't even jump out of bed one day. And, I believe a large majority of grievers start their journey to their "new normal" this way too. The change is so slight, it is unnoticeable at first. It isn't until you turn around one day much later—and you really see how far you've come—that you realize how low you truly were.

That right there is why books don't {or can't} tell you how to start back up from the "rock bottom" of your pit. It is such a gradual shift that to the naked eye it goes completely unnoticed.

One day, several years into my grief journey, I woke and looked at my calendar {to see what the absolute bare minimum I had to do that day was}. There was nothing pressing that had to be done {when you work for yourself, you get to take some liberties}, so I debated even getting out of bed at all that day; it was then I realized I was living my life just waiting to die. I was doing the bare minimum to get from one nap to the next {grief had taken my ability to actually *sleep*}, before I could take the ultimate dirt nap.

In case you weren't sure, that is not the way to live your life— being miserable and making everyone around you miserable. So, I had to decide. I could either opt for the dirt nap, or I could try to do something, ANYTHING, with my life. So, I got out of bed, *and* I took a shower {putting on makeup and fixing my hair was still too much to handle but again, baby steps}. Then the next day I thought to myself, "I did it yesterday; let's see if I can do it again." Before you know it, there I was showering. Every day. {Well, almost.}

All this said, I do believe there are a couple wrong ways to grieve. If you feel like you're going to physically harm yourself, or anyone else, that might not be the right way to process your emotions. I strongly encourage you to seek professional help (more on my struggle and experience with professional help in When in Doubt, Get More Information on page 205).

Now it's your turn. You decide how you'd like to move forward:

Still think you're digging your pit or feel like you want to still be digging? **Turn the page** and remember: **Don't Believe the Things You Tell Yourself...**

Do you still believe there's a "right way to grieve"? Maybe you better **Take Me to Church**? Turn to **page 89**.

Wanna know more about my baby steps {and get some ideas for your own}? Turn to **page 185** for **Write it Down and Work it Out, B!tch**.

There's a difference between **Not Wanting to Be Alive** vs. Wanting to Be Dead. I think I figured it out the hard way...more than once. Turn to **page 171** to read on.

DON'T BELIEVE THE THINGS YOU TELL YOURSELF...

...this is really just a friendly reminder...

...something I need to be reminded of on a weekly {okay, daily} basis...

> *Don't believe the things you tell yourself when you're alone, afraid, hungry, late at night, or sad. Your mind is not your friend right now.*

Our brains have been trained after hundreds of thousands of years to search for the worst-case scenario {so we can plan for it and hopefully outlive it}. Basically, it's survival of the fittest.

A couple of my all-time favorite sayings are: {Shameless plug: go check out @SharingSolace on Instagram if you like these quotes and want more. I post inspiring quotes several times a week over there.}

- Don't buy from late-night infomercials and don't trust your late-night thoughts.

- Don't believe the things you tell yourself when you are sad and alone.

Anyone else remember the '90s song by Lit—"I am my Own Worst Enemy"? (No, just me…mmmokaythen) The song is about a guy who continues to get drunk and ruin his relationship with a girl…but these lyrics have always stood out to me and I find them very fitting:

It's no surprise to me I am my own worst enemy
Cause every now and then I kick the living sh!t out of me

Right now, in the depths of your grief, is the time you are your own worst enemy. You are beating yourself up and blaming yourself for things that were outside of your control.

QUIT TRYING TO COME UP WITH REASONS TO MAKE THIS YOUR FAULT!

If we let ourselves, we will go down the rabbit hole {I've told you; I did} and we convince ourselves this tragedy is just leading up to the next one. I mean, if everything happens for a reason, then this happened so we can be prepared for something much worse to happen…Just around the corner. We're just waiting for the other shoe to drop…

(And/) Or, you will find ways to blame yourself for *this* tragedy—if only you had been a few minutes earlier, if you hadn't forgotten your cell phone, if you had reminded them to be careful, if you had put away the mower, if you had turned off the oven… We could play this game all day long.

You DID love them enough {and you told them so}, you DID make all the right decisions, and you DID say the right words.

Do not believe yourself right now. You are your own worst enemy.

Now it's your turn. You decide where to go:

I give you permission to have self-compassion on your grief journey. Give yourself the same **Permission**. Turn to **page 51** for that reminder.

Turn to **page 165** and **Stop Suffer Shopping**; you're going nowhere fast, and it won't give you the same "retail therapy high" that the mall will.

"De Nile" ain't just a river in Egypt. It's also one of my "favorite" emotions. Read on: **Denial—My Personal Story** is on **the next page**.

DENIAL - MY PERSONAL STORY

The day after I was given the potentially earth-shattering, world-rocking news by my OB—that my baby was going to die {if it wasn't already dead} was more of the "same old, same old" {ha!}. Multiple intense ultrasounds {You know, the wand kind. If you don't, you're lucky} and an MRI. If you've never had an MRI, I wouldn't particularly recommend it. They strip you down, pump your body full of some sort of fluid that makes you feel like you're constantly pottying yourself, "rip" you away from the only other person who even remotely understands what you're going through, and shove you in a big metal tube for sixty to ninety minutes, while reminding you every twelve seconds to hold perfectly still or they'll have to start all over again.

Now, I don't know about you, but in my experience, it's nearly impossible to sob uncontrollably about your "dying before it's even lived" baby while holding perfectly still for over an hour {or, you know, maybe ten minutes; time continued to elude me}.

Once the MRI was done, they confirmed the worst possible news: our little bundle of joy would not survive—if the child even made it to its own birthday. We had two options: continue with the pregnancy as long as it was safe for me (knowing that a classic C-section was in my future) or terminate at thirty-two-plus weeks (which meant traveling to another state hundreds of miles away—where it wasn't illegal to do so). After getting all the information and weighing all the pros and cons, we decided to continue with the pregnancy for as long as we could, for as long as it was "reasonably safe" for my health, and for as long as we could keep our little one alive.

──────── Hopping Up on My Soapbox Here ────────

I'm not going to mince words, and I feel it needs to be said. I am Pro-Choice. And, I am Pro-Choice at all stages of pregnancy. While I don't know that I had a firm opinion before Madelyn came into my life, I definitely have one now. (All that being said, termination/abortion/interruption/whatever you choose to call it is not a form of contraception. There are pills and patches and foams and all kinds of stuff for that. Don't be silly. Wrap your willy.)

I've spent the last ten-plus years of my life in the "baby loss" arena. I've had the opportunity to meet hundreds {if not thousands} of amazingly strong loss mamas. I've met women who've lost their pregnancy "naturally." I've met women who've had outside forces end their pregnancy. And, I've met women who've had to make the choice to end their pregnancy. But, I have never met a woman that had to contemplate a termination at any point in their pregnancy (myself included) and chose to take that decision lightly. It is literally a life and death decision for (at least) two people.

There are legitimate and severe medical, physical, and psychological consequences to consider and evaluate. Even though I chose to continue my pregnancy to the "bitter end"—I honestly cannot judge someone who chooses another option. Neither option is good. Neither option is right.

But something didn't make sense to me. Every professional we met with was amazed our baby's issues hadn't been found earlier in the pregnancy. It *should* have been spotted at an earlier ultrasound—like at the first twelve-week ultrasound or the twenty-week anatomy scan. Why were our baby's issues just being spotted now, at thirty-two weeks?

If they didn't find issues all those weeks ago, why were they being found now? Something *has* to be wrong with the ultrasound machine or the MRI equipment. The specialists must not be able to see it all. Everything in my belly is just so cramped—with all the arms and legs and torso and such— the specialists had to be reading the scans and printouts incorrectly.

Or, more likely {because this child is its mother's child}, our baby must be playing a trick. Yup, that's it!! The baby thought this pregnancy was too easy on me, so it wanted to throw a wrench in the works. Just like our baby's mama, this baby was gonna be a feisty one and wanted to make that fact known from the get-go…

Now it's your turn. How do you want to proceed?

Still want more of my story? I promise, this ain't no M. Night Shyamalan movie; there's no unexpected twist, nobody sees dead people. What you think is going to happen really happens. Okay, you had your warning: turn to **page 101** for **Anger—My Personal Story.**

Are you as anxious as I am just reading this? Need a reminder to chill out? **Turn the page** to **Just F'ing Breathe.**

Think this story is total cr@p? Yeah, well I'll tell you what's what! Turn to **page 197** to **Go Duck Yourself.**

JUST F'ING BREATHE

That's it. **Just. F'ing. Breathe.** When you find yourself getting worked up, anxious, depressed, or worried, focus on your breathing.

...in through your nose...1.2.3...

...out through your mouth...1.2.3.4.5.6...

...in through your nose...1.2.3...

...out through your mouth...1.2.3.4.5.6...

...in through your nose...1.2.3...

...out through your mouth...1.2.3.4.5.6...

Give yourself nice looooooong exhales to release the toxins, stress, and worry. This is a yoga technique that I've pulled into my everyday life.

Have you ever noticed that when you get worked up your breath quickens, and you tend to have long inhales and short exhales? No? Have you ever noticed that when you're having a "really good think" you tend to sigh? No? Me neither until I really started paying attention. Those breathing patterns are your body reacting to your mind and emotions. {Someone once told me "your cells eavesdrop on your thoughts," and it's so true. They just feed off each other.}

Longer, deeper exhales are calming. Which is why when your mind is at ease you tend to sigh. If you find yourself on edge, try "tricking" your body into calming down with long, deep, tranquil breaths.

…in through your nose…1.2.3…

…out through your mouth…1.2.3.4.5.6…

…in through your nose…1.2.3…

…out through your mouth…1.2.3.4.5.6…

…in through your nose…1.2.3…

…out through your mouth…1.2.3.4.5.6…

—————————————— Side Note ——————————————

It's scientifically proven that no one in the history of **ever** has calmed down by just being told to calm down. If you suggest it to someone else, you're more likely to get kicked in the shins than you are getting the other person to chill out.

There you go, when you find your tummy tied up in knots, focus on your breathing. Now you may go on with your regularly scheduled life.

Now it's your turn. You pick where you wanna go:

Have you forgotten that **Any Loss is Grieveable?**
Turn to **page 45** for a quick refresher.

There are certain things you need as a
griever. **The Needs of Mourning** will
explain each to you. **Turn the page.**

There Is No Right Way to Grieve—you do you (boo).
Grieve and mourn how you choose. Turn to **page 55.**

THE NEEDS OF MOURNING

** Hold on to your handkerchiefs friends, this is the
big, main "book learnin'" story. It'll probably feel a
little stale, but it's all really good information. I'll do
my best to make it as entertaining as possible **

Did you know that grieving and mourning are different?

"Grieving" is the emotional, internal response to a loss.
"Mourning" is the outward display of that grief. Being sad is
grieving; crying is mourning.

I don't believe you can (healthily) have one without the
other. If you're not grieving, there's really nothing to outwardly mourn. But, if you're grieving a loss and don't (or
can't) externally express signs of mourning— that's where
the issues begin.

Not allowing yourself to outwardly mourn (share stories,
journal, cry, allow yourself to feel your feels, generally get
your feelings out of your physical body, etc.) is what keeps you
from beginning to heal. In fact, author Cheryl Richardson
(she's one of Oprah's BFFs) says, "People start to heal the
moment they feel heard." By not moving toward mourning
(and therefore healing), you're just teaching yourself it's okay

to bottle up your emotions…and at some point you'll explode like a can of soda kicked down the road. I promise, that's what happens. {Been there, done that, have the T-shirt.}

If you haven't heard about Dr. Alan D. Wolfelt along your grief journey, I'd like to introduce you {"My friend, Dr. Wolfelt; Dr. Wolfelt, my friend."} This guy has spent the last three-plus decades educating, researching, and counseling on grief. He runs the Center for Loss and Life Transition in Colorado too. I encourage you to read his book *The Wilderness of Grief: Finding Your Way*. It's a concise book dispelling many of the misconceptions of grief. The chapters are short, and you can pick it up and put it down over and over again {the perfect kinda book for "one of us"}. We'll come back to good ol' Alan in a moment.

Robert Frost said, "The best way out is always through." While you know my take is that you never get "out" of grief, I still find this quote fitting. You don't get to "skirt the edges" of grief and expect to begin to heal in a meaningful way. You gotta go right smack dab through the middle of your grief {feeling all the feels and exploring all the painful thoughts} to make progress toward healing.

I do like how Dr. Wolfelt[2] says that to mourn is to "actively participate" in your grief journey—the key word here is ACTIVELY. He also says there are six "markers" all mourners will experience on their path. Now that doesn't mean your grief journey will not be uniquely personal and intense—it

---

2   Wolfelt, Ph.D., Alan D. *The Journey Through Grief: The Six Needs of Mourning*. Center for Loss, 2016.

more means these are the basic human needs of grief: like food, water, shelter, and companionship. This is what he believes needs to happen for you to be "actively participating" in your grief:

──────────────── Side Note ────────────────

Dr. Wolfelt specifically writes about loss via a death, but I believe these needs apply to all loss and all grief. If you are mourning the loss of something other than a death, please remove the word "death" and replace it with something more fitting (I've tried to help you out and do that where I can already).

NEED 1: ACKNOWLEDGING THE REALITY OF THE DEATH (OR LOSS)

Confront your loss. Allow yourself to realize the reality of the loss. This (insert appropriate noun: person, job, pet, dream, etc.) will never be a physical part of your life again. You'll probably find yourself replaying memories (both good and bad) over and over again in your mind. If there are questions or "unsolved mysteries" around your loss, you'll probably spend a fair bit of time thinking through every minute detail, wondering if something could have been done differently.

Please do spend time, *constructively*, reliving the events leading up to and shortly after your loss. As much as this will hurt your heart, it is vital to the mourning process. It helps to make your loss more real (which, again, is how you begin to heal).

This need, along with the other five, may require you circling back to pay attention to it from time to time (weeks, months, or maybe even years later). This is not a clear-cut path with a finish line. Give yourself patience and self-compassion to tend to your needs as much as you need. Don't beat yourself up because you're not "where you should be." You're exactly where you need to be in your journey; it just might not match with your {or society's} expectations.

NEED 2: EMBRACING THE PAIN OF YOUR LOSS

Feel your freakin' feels. Pain and sorrow are going to be your new BFFs for a little while. I know you probably don't want to hear that; in fact, it's a million times easier (at first) to push those feelings deeeeeep down to where you've all but forgotten about them.

You're not expected to feel ALL your feelings in one sitting. Take them in bite-size chunks when you can. (You don't always get to choose how and when your feelings will hit you, but, when you can, do it in pieces.) Finding distractions from the pain is perfectly acceptable from time to time. One of my favorite ways to distract myself is to play card games. Rummy, Go Fish, and Kings on the Corners are all great go-to games. You know how to play them from childhood, and they involve very little mental capacity. You can space in and out and still have an idea of what is going on in the game. {You're going to "space in and out" anyway; you might as well embrace it.}

"Doing great," "Staying strong," "Looking good," and all that other junk is just that, JUNK. It's not something to strive for. You're actually doing "future you" more harm by not embracing your emotions and feelings in the present. You don't need to "keep up appearances" for yourself or anyone else. Be real and authentic.

NEED 3: REMEMBERING THE PERSON WHO DIED (OR THE THING THAT'S GONE)

The "great" philosopher and rapper, Macklemore, in the song "Glorious," once said "I heard you die twice, once when they bury you in the grave. And the second time is the last time that somebody mentions your name." Honestly, I've found that Banksy is credited with the sentiment and another citing where it's said to be an old Jewish saying…it doesn't really matter who said it. It's just plain true.

There will be people in your life that will want to "help" you by removing the physical signs of your loss (pictures, souvenirs, clothing, etc.) and will try to take away your memories as quickly as possible. They think they are doing what's best for you. Maybe they want to help you move out of your home or take the kibble bowl out of the kitchen. While this is all well and good, it's only good when it's *your* idea and on *your* time frame. Take time to tell stories (to yourself through journaling or vlogging or to others through conversation). Capture your memories (good and bad) and hold them close to your heart.

The more you choose to remember and share these stories, the easier (and more fulfilling) it will become to share about your loss. Hopefully, one day when you're sharing your memories, you'll notice your tears of pain have become tears of happy remembrance.

NEED 4: DEVELOPING A NEW SELF-IDENTITY

Self-identity is a tough one. Especially if you identified yourself in a certain way for a very long time. We often define ourselves based on our relationships with others: Mother, Father, Sister, Brother, Husband, Wife, Son, Daughter…and it can all change just LIKE*THAT.

Not only do we all self-identify, but society also defines you by the relationships they can see. This concept has caused particular difficulty for me, personally. I AM a mother. {Period.} I just don't change poopy diapers, or wake up for midnight feedings, nor am I a Girl Scout troop leader. I still want to present the best example I can for my daughter and make her proud; others just can't see with their eyes what I feel in my heart.

Oftentimes, after a loss, while in the process of finding that new identity, we tend to regress. Like a kiddo working to become independent, you can get frustrated, irritated, and sometimes feel helpless. On top of those helpless feelings, you *also* have to fill the role/s that were once held by others {someone still needs to mow the lawn and fold the laundry}, which can become extra emotionally draining (in addition to the already draining effects of grief).

As you work toward finding your new identity, you may find new aspects of your life that you enjoy or consider yourself good at {who knew you could change the car's oil or bake a beautiful soufflé?}. You will almost definitely find you're a more compassionate and empathetic person. Developing your new self-identity makes me think of the platitude {even though you know I think platitudes are cr@p} "If it doesn't kill you, it makes you stronger."

NEED 5: SEARCHING FOR MEANING

"How?" and "Why?" are going to be about ninety percent of the questions you ask yourself—over and over and over. I can almost promise you will deeply examine a lot of the beliefs you formerly held as truths. If you are a spiritual person, you may either grow closer to or veer away from your faith.

You will not only question the meaning behind your loss but also the meaning of life completely. "Why did this happen to me? What is my purpose on this Earth if it is not to ___?"

All of these questions and feelings are normal while you grieve. Please allow yourself to ask those questions of yourself...*and* explore your answers. But understand that your answers might not be the "right" answers for everyone {there may not even be a "right answer" to your question}. Be critical of the things you used to hold as "truths." For me, personally, I turned away from the organized religion I grew up with but became much more faithful in the process. {And because I was able to come to terms with that previous disconnect in my life, I am a much happier person today.} Read my take on this in Take Me to Church? on page 89.

You will not find the answers to your questions overnight; maybe you'll never find an answer to some of them. You will, however, start to find YOUR meaning {and *your* silver linings}. *That* is the true goal.

NEED 6: RECEIVING ONGOING SUPPORT FROM OTHERS

You're not gonna be able to do this alone, so please don't try. You need quantity *and* quality when it comes to support. Meaningful support from your social circle typically ends shortly after your loss (three to six months is pretty standard). That is why you can't only rely on friends and family. Please {please, please, please, please, please} consider finding a therapist, mentor, or other grief professional to talk to regularly and/or a constructive support group; they have walked in your shoes. They understand grief is a never-ending path. And, they will offer you the love and support you need long after your friends and family have moved forward with their own lives.

————————————— Side Note —————————————

Support groups can be tricky to navigate. If I have one bit of advice for you, it's "keep looking." You need to find one that resonates with you and your unique grief and which is also willing to support and challenge you to heal. Misery loves company, and some support groups become "Grief Ghettos."

————————— Side Note to the Side Note —————————

I am a HUGE proponent of seeking out professional support: someone you pay to listen to you b!tch. You don't have to feel bad about bogarting the conversation or only talking about what you want to talk about. That's the POINT of it! You do need to be open to receiving the professional advice as well…If you're not open to receive professional advice, then I suggest you visit the last story option below.

I've said it before, and it's worth saying again. **YOU DO NOT GET OVER GRIEF.** You learn to live with it, hold it, carry it…it becomes a part of you as you find your way toward your new normal. Once you are able to reconcile with your new normal, only then will you be able to move forward with your life with a renewed sense of meaning and purpose.

Now it's your turn. You decide how to move forward:

Not all support groups turn into **Grief Ghettos**…but they can if you're not careful and selective. Turn to **page 159** to see what I mean.

You don't get over grief. {Do I sound like a broken record?} You learn to internalize it. You become stronger. And, you learn to carry it better. Learn why **Grief Is a Broken Rib** by turning to **page 219**.

Do these needs not quite resonate with you yet? That's okay. **This Might Not Be Your Time.** You might not be ready to move forward just yet. You must do this on your own schedule. **Turn the page** to learn more.

THIS MIGHT NOT
BE YOUR TIME

...and that is perfectly okay...

Not everything you read in this book will resonate with you right now {maybe some will never resonate with you}. You could be too early in your journey—or much further down the path. Or, maybe there's a third option. Maybe you just haven't heard it at the right time, in the right way.

You know how you can pass the same billboard every day for a year, and then one day see it's an advert of a doctor, and you realize you need to go to the doctor, so you make an appointment with your doctor? Or, how someone suggests something to you and ten seconds later you suggest the exact same thing, like it was your idea? THAT'S what I mean. You might just need to listen to this a few times before you actually *hear* it.

There's a small piece of your brain near the spinal cord called the reticular activating system (or RAS for short). It acts like a filter between the conscious and unconscious parts of your brain. Just got a new red car? Now you notice every red car on the road. Think you are always behind? You WILL always be running late—because you're focusing on it. Think you'll never be happy again? Guess what, it's going to be hard for you to find happiness. Another way to think about this is "what you focus on expands." You gotta focus on the good stuff to *get* the good stuff.

If this, or any book, resonates with your heart, I suggest you keep it around and continue to read it over and over {ya know, like some do with…say…the Bible…wink}. Make it part of your own special resource library. Reread those books cover to cover, a chapter here and a chapter there, skip around to the "good bits"; whatever you need. Just keep the resources that speak to you (and don't be afraid to dig into them again and again on the tough days).

Another great book which illustrates this concept (that I continue to read over and over and I always get something new out of it each time) is *The Alchemist*[3] by Paulo Coelho. It's an easy, parable-style story that illustrates just how "ready" you need to be in life to get what you want. It's the tale of a young shepherd boy who travels around the world just to find out that what he's been missing has been right in front of him the whole time. If he were "lucky," he would have found it much earlier in life, but he also would have missed out on many adventures and lessons along the way.

That book means so much to me and has shaped so much of my post-Madelyn life, that I want to share my experience of the book with you. This is not me "Cliff's note-ing" the book,

---

3   Coelho, Paulo. *The Alchemist: A Fable About Following Your Dream.*
     Harper San Francisco, 1988.

mind you; you'll still have to read it yourself. It is more the story of how I came to read the book and why I believe it should be on everyone's "must read" list.

"One uponce a time" {as my three-year-old husband would say to his mama years and years ago}, I was living in a country where English wasn't their native language. While I was still able to communicate with others...a little bit...it was anxiety inducing to do so {this is before the time of smart phones and there was no such thing as Google translate}. I found I secluded myself unless absolutely necessary. It was just easier to stay inside and play Farmville on my desktop computer while watching DVDs {again, a long time ago} than it was to be out "amongst the living."

Sometimes, when sitting alone in the corner got too boring, I would read. {I could devour an entire book in a single sitting.} I ran out of books often {there was no such thing as Kindle at the time, and how many times in a row can you really read *Harry Potter* or *Twilight* before trying to become a wizarding vampire yourself?}

Down the road was a used English bookstore. When I ran out of things to read, I would send the hubby out to get more books {I really did become a hermit}. He'd bring back a few books and I'd immediately read them cover to cover whether they were good or not, then send him back out for more.

Flash forward to about 2012. We'd moved home and Madelyn had already been on this Earth and left us... I was unpacking books that hadn't quite made it to the bookshelf in our new house when I spot a book I don't remember (and I'd read EVERYTHING in that box—multiple times). I stopped unpacking to read the first chapter or so and then shelved it...meh...

A few months later, on that same bookshelf, a book I don't recognize catches my eye. I pull it out and set it on my desk to read...it sits there for a while...probably a year or more. The book is still sitting under a pile of papers and junk when my business coach tells me about a story I should really consider reading. Later that same week, I hear about that same story from three other unrelated people {you can probably figure out where I'm going with this...}.

After I've been told four times in a week I should read this one particular book, I decide to hop on Amazon and see about placing an order {by now Amazon, smartphones, and Kindles are the wave of the future}. The book cover looks strangely familiar. So, I dig through the bookshelf—just to make sure we don't already have it {that's a thing that happens a lot in our house—wanting to buy books I already own} and there it is. *The Alchemist* sitting on my desk collecting dust under a pile of junk, just waiting to be read.

It's now been several years and several mentions that I've intended to read this book, so I sit down and read it...cover to cover, nonstop right there on my office floor. Finishing the book, I flip to the inside front cover to see when it was published {It felt like it could have been published hundreds of years ago...and also yesterday...} and right there, next to the "©1988' is "3CHF."

Holy crap on a cracker! I bought this book when I felt like I was at my lowest of lows {little did I know, right?}. When I was just biding my time before I could come home. That means I had to have picked the book up and put it down at least a dozen times over there, and again at least a dozen more here!

I just couldn't get into the story before. I couldn't hear the message until I was READY to hear the message—and I wasn't ready yet. The universe {or maybe it was Madelyn} conspired *with* me, so that when I finally *heard* the message of the book it aligned perfectly with when I was *ready to hear* that message.

I could now take it to heart and get my booty moving! The message would have been completely lost on me if I had read those words any time before when I actually did {and clearly there were many times the message could have been lost on me with all the times I picked up and put down the book!}.

Reading that book led me to start going to the gym, to start journaling, and to start Sharing Solace. I'm not saying you will have the same experience with the book that I did; what I'm really saying is there is a time and a place for everything.

It might not be *your* time or *your* place, but don't ignore the nudges the universe gives you. If your brain wanders to something multiple times, or someone brings something up over and over again...maybe, just maybe, something up there is trying to guide you—trying to push you in the direction you're intended to go. Take ten minutes and explore, go down that path. Let the universe help you...help the universe!

The flip side of that coin is that sometimes, no matter how hard you try, not everything will happen on your timeline. You can push and push and push to do something, but if it's not "supposed" to happen in the amount of time you want it to, it just won't. "Forcing it" is like putting a square peg in a round hole—it just won't work. Sometimes, you can do everything humanly possible, and then you just have to give it over to your higher power.

Sometimes, you just need to have patience with the process. The universe conspires with you if you allow it.

Now it's your turn. Where do you want to go?

Wanna hear about this gyming and journaling thing I mentioned above; the turning point in my life that *The Alchemist* started? Turn to **page 185** for **Write It Down and Work It Out, B!tch.**

Do you feel like sometimes the universe is conspiring against you (not with you)? Boy, I know that feeling!! Turn to **page 201** for **This Is Not a Test.**

Or, think this "universe" thing is a bunch of made-up phooey? **Turn the page** and **Take Me to Church?**

TAKE ME TO CHURCH?

Like my Letter from the Author said: grief support books, historically, have either been "fact and figure" based or "Jesus is the supreme being of the entire universe" based. I think I've pretty well proven this book is not, even a little bit, either.

I'll be honest with you. I grew up Catholic, went to Sunday school, got baptized and confirmed, and all that other good stuff. I even got married in a Catholic church, but I never really considered myself a devout follower...more of a C&E kinda girl.

When we found out Madelyn would die, we went to our family church. This was the church both my husband and I grew up attending {his mother played the piano and sang every Sunday morning for yeeeeeeeeeeeeeears}. We went to our longtime parish priest to ask for guidance. His response?

"Call the office when you're ready to schedule the funeral."

"...um, okay..."

Yup, that was it. No compassion, no "Jesus has a plan"...not even a pity prayer or insincere condolence. Just "let us know when we can start dealing with the logistics."

It was basically then and there that I realized organized religion was not for me. (Madelyn did have a full Catholic funeral—at a different church—and we tried our hardest to "get back into it"…but my heart just wasn't there.) My heart was already bleeding out of control, and "my" religion ground sand into the open wound. I felt like it was the final straw that broke the camel's back.

All that being said, I HAVE to believe there is a higher power. Call it God, Jesus, Buddha, Energy, Supreme Being, Mother Earth, your Priestess, the Universe…call it little green men from Mars for all I care! There have been too many serendipitous coincidences in my life to NOT believe there is something out there helping and guiding me. Honestly? I like to think it's my Maddie up there lining all my ducks up in a row for me {because my "ducks" down here on Earth are actually squirrels—and they're all at a rave}.

I just couldn't imagine Madelyn's short eight-hour life on Earth being all there is for her. I believe her physical body just couldn't handle the smartness of her brain and awesomeness of her soul…

Okay. But here's the deal {bringing this around full circle}… Religion, politics, and pretty much all other opinions are like, well… {insert your favorite word for male genitalia here}. You can have one—that's great. You can even be super proud of how big and rigid yours is. But, the second you whip it out and start shoving it in my face, we're gonna have a problem.

While I do seem to have a rather engorged "Private Johnson" from time to time, I do my best to keep it under wraps. This is probably the most you will hear about my personal views in one sitting {stories and anecdotes aside}. I think you've seen, this will not be a book about "praying yourself to positivity," nor is it about "logic-ing your way to happiness."

Like my opinion, or not. Take it or leave it. I don't care to have opinions being crammed down my throat, so I won't do that to you either.

Basically, this is a long-winded and convoluted way for me to say I've found my solace {in an unconventional way} and I hope that you can too. There's no right way to do that, though. Maybe it's through your faith and religion, maybe it's through logic, maybe it's through your divine inner essence. Find your way to make peace with your experiences and don't let anyone tell you it's wrong.

Now it's your turn. You decide how you'd like to move forward:

Wanna go to a different kinda church? **Turn the page** for **I Am Your Grief Guru.**

Think my soapbox isn't quite tall enough yet and wanna see if I can get a little higher? Turn to **page 125** for **Grief Shaming and Victim Blaming.**

Maybe this is a little over-the-top for you. Or, not what you believe in {or were expecting}. Take a quick U-turn to **page 69** and remember to **Just F'ing Breathe.**

I AM YOUR GRIEF GURU

———

Okay. Not really. I say this soooooo tongue in cheek I'm surprised you can even understand what I'm saying through all the mumbling.

When you feel lost—like you do in debilitating grief—all you want is some reprieve. You want someone or something to make it all better—to "kiss the boo-boo" and apply a bandage to your exposed and bloody heart. You want someone to tell you what to do, how to feel, and how to make it all go away. You *need* them to just do it. To make all the hurt, sadness, sorrow, and lethargy disappear.

You assume the people who have walked the path before you (me included) have it all figured out and have all the magic answers. That's bullsh!t. They don't. We don't. We don't have the foggiest idea what we're doing either. We all put our pants on one leg at a time. No one is a Guru of Grief; there is no amount of studying, experiencing, experimenting, researching, or interviewing that can make you the be all, end all expert of grief.

"Guru" is such an overused term in today's society. I think it just makes people sound idiotic {unless it is actually a term used in your religion—that's perfectly acceptable and encouraged}. People are not "marketing gurus," or "social media ninjas," or "physiology rock stars," or any other ridiculous word pairing. The term has been bastardized from its original meaning. It's dumb. Don't be dumb.

──────────────── Side Note ────────────────
It reminds me of when "build your own" frozen yogurt shops were all the rage. Did you ever notice there was a formula for the names? Color Noun. Think about it: Orange Leaf, Pink Berry, Red Mango, Peach Wave...

For a while, the same thing was kinda happening with salespeople: what you sell + racially insensitive generalization = what you call yourself at networking events.
───

The Oxford definition of Guru is: in Hinduism and Buddhism—a spiritual teacher, especially one who imparts initiation (initiation: the action of admitting someone into a secret or obscure society or group, typically with a ritual).

For some reason, though, I really "like" the term "Grief Guru" here {maybe it's the alliteration, maybe it's the complete oxymoron}. This term is absurd on so many levels:

1. Who in their right mind wants to WILLINGLY LEARN grief? And then, actually want to TEACH it to others?
2. The idea of being an expert in grief is dumb. The idea of using "guru" out of context is dumb. Put them together: double dumb.
3. Each person's story and journey is uniquely theirs. How can someone else lead them along a path if there is really

no path to begin with? Only YOU can be the expert of your own grief {everyone else will just try to tell you what they think is best for you}—you're the only one who knows how to handle each moment.

4. No one "masters" grief…or at least I hope no one HAS to master grief—that's just too much grief. If you do "truly master grief," that means you get used to it. If you're used to grief, that means it begins to not matter to you. If grief and death and loss begin to not matter to you, then I think you might have some bigger problems to look into—like you're becoming a heartless robot.

I do believe you learn to carry your grief with you in a way that is as unobtrusive as possible. (See Grocery Bag Grief on page 245.)

There is one piece of the definition of "guru" that I do think applies to grief: admitting someone into a secret or obscure society or group, typically with a ritual.

First, what's more ritualistic than a funeral?

Second, we, as the mourning, are part of an obscure society. We are banished to the outskirts of conversations until we can "learn to behave normally." Until we learn to brush our grief and sadness under the rug and hide it from others. What "non-grievers" don't understand is that THIS is our new normal. Our grief has forever changed us, like a caterpillar into a butterfly. We are learning to fly {though at first it will feel like we're being buried alive}.

I, for one, prefer the "outskirts of conversations." Fine, look away when you see me coming, pretend you don't notice me as I say "hello." The relationships I have now—with others "like me"—are fuller, more meaningful, and far more real than the relationships I had with those I only spoke to about rainbows, the weather, and puppy dogs.

What I'm ultimately trying to say is don't go looking for your Grief Guru. And, don't trust anyone who says they are a Grief Guru. Because they just don't exist. What you're really looking for, IMHO, is a "Grief Sherpa." Someone who can help to guide you along the journey (not tell you how), someone who will walk alongside you to pick you up and dust you off, someone who will help you carry the weight when it feels unbearable. "Grief Sherpas" do exist – present company included. And those are the people and organizations you need to seek out.

Dr. Wolfelt calls this "companioning the grieving." I want to take it one step further. I believe it is every seasoned griever's duty to help guide those newer to the journey. It is our responsibility to provide an ear to bend, a shoulder to cry on, and a nonjudgmental embrace. We are here to provide support where there may be none otherwise and to give counsel when requested. It takes no degree or license to companion the grieving. The only true requirement is to be on this grief journey longer than your counterpart.

So, no. I am not your Grief Guru—but it is my great pleasure to be your Grief Sherpa.

Now it's your turn. You decide where to go next:

Want to know the right way to grieve? You're probably doing it wrong {wink}. Turn to **page 55** because **There Is No Right Way to Grieve.**

Does this idea make you angry? Does your loss and grief make you angry? **Turn the page** for **Anger—My Personal Story.**

Think you have a "grief problem"? Please remember that **Grief Is Not a Problem.** Turn to **page 139** to find out what I mean.

ANGER - MY PERSONAL STORY

———

The fifteen days between the specialist's official diagnosis and our angel's birthday were a blurry whirlwind: meeting with doctors multiple times a week to make sure baby wasn't dead…yet. Meeting with hospice workers to get everything in order for when that time did come. Spending the few precious moments we did have with our little one, getting to know them and their little (and yet so very BIG) personality, and trying to make the necessary "arrangements" as we could.

We now knew that our "happy and healthy" request was not going to be granted, so we wanted to get to know our child as much as possible while we still had that opportunity—we asked to know our baby's sex. She was a little girl. We named her Madelyn Elizabeth Webster. Her name was special to us and was the name we had picked long before we got our "diagnosis." We spent hours just talking to her: about how much we loved her, wanted her, how we couldn't wait to see her, how we knew she was feisty like her mama and smart like her daddy. We told her about all the plans we had for her and read her all the Dr. Seuss books we {and she} could handle.

She loved *Green Eggs and Ham*—and her daddy would read it to her over and over and over again, all in one sitting. In true "daddy form," each time the book was read, words were left out and pages skipped entirely…to the point, at the end, the book became just:

"Ham?"
"Nah."

"Ham?"
"No."

"Ham?"
"Okay."

Madelyn's birthday came six and a half weeks early via a classical C-section on May 19, 2010. She was surrounded by only love and was barely put down her entire life {the doctor insisted we get her weight, which required her to be set down long enough for the scale to register}. Her whole extended family was there to welcome this beautiful little girl into the world; with her cute button nose and her mama's blue eyes. I felt so lucky and honored that she was able to stay alive long enough for everyone to meet her. She was the epitome of perfection {granted I'm a little bit biased}. Ten fingers, ten toes. The only minor indication that anything was wrong was that her head was extra large {you know, for all those smarts her daddy gave her}.

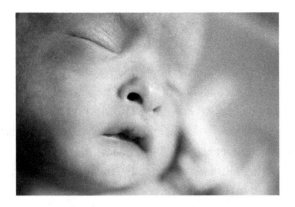

We loved her, and loved her, and loved her...like there was no tomorrow; because there *was* no tomorrow. We gave her all the love a mother and father can give their child—and we squeezed it into eight short hours. The only wish I had during those fleeting eight hours was that I would have liked to have been more coherent. My C-section led to massive amounts of morphine to manage the pain. Coupled with severe dehydration {only ice chips} and sixteen days without sleep, my "memories" of my daughter are an entangled mess of *actual* memories and made up memories I pieced together from pictures, videos, and stories from others.

The next day, May 20, 2010, we said goodbye to our baby girl for the last time. In the early morning hours before sunrise she died, smiling and cooing, in my arms.

Even after death, our darling daughter was so loved. The grandmas shopped for her funeral outfit and personalized it with her name. Grandpa, a woodworker, built her a tiny little coffin. And her mommy and daddy worked tirelessly to plan a meaningful and special service. For someone so extraordinary, it was the very least we could do for her.

Her service was my "final" outward act of love for my daughter. It had to be special, and I stretched myself beyond my capability to make it so—physically and mentally. The day after her services, I was put on bed rest because my C-section incision had reopened, and I had to have a home health nurse come to the house two times a day to "pack the wound" so it didn't get infected {bleck}.

While it is absolutely amazing {and disgusting} what the human body can do, I felt vindicated in my pain. If I could *prove* I was suffering physically, I was *allowed* to continue to suffer emotionally. The longer I was outwardly suffering, the longer I could continue to suffer inside. In many ways, I never wanted my scars to heal.

And that led to its own unique challenges. Because I couldn't physically do much {I was allowed to climb the stairs once a day to shower, if absolutely necessary}, my mind had plenty of time to wander and go down the "what if rabbit hole" (no amount of staring at the TV could prevent it).

What did I do wrong? Why was I cursed? Why was I unable to do the *"ONE THING"* women are biologically intended to do? I made up story after story of how karma had come back around, or I had spent too much time mourning the loss of my aunt and uncle, or set the computer on my belly in bed one too many times, or ate too many tortilla chips with salsa and mac n' cheese...

I had the "chicken or the egg" conversation with myself a million times a day. If "everything happens for a reason," then did Madelyn die because Kent and Jane needed someone to care for? Or, because I knew I was pregnant with Madelyn before the accident, did I kill Kent and Jane because my Madelyn needed someone to care for her when her mama couldn't? (These unanswerable questions still haunt me to this very day.)

After the traditional Catholic funeral services, we felt it was best to have our Madelyn cremated {feel free, judge away}. She continues to live on my nightstand with her pink stuffed turtle, and I say "goodnight" to her every night. {When we travel and can't take her with us, she and her pink turtle go to Grandma's house.} While I know not everyone agrees with our decision for cremation, I just couldn't bring myself to bury her in the cold, hard ground. The ground is for grandparents. It is for people who have lived long lives and are able to take care of themselves (both on Earth and in the afterlife). Madelyn is just a baby; she needs to be with her mama, and I need to take care of her. But I couldn't do that if she was far away, six feet underground.

What felt like months later, long after my incision healed and I was able to drive myself around town again, we received the autopsy results. I still don't know if it is, in fact, "standard protocol" to perform an autopsy on all babies that die, or if that was just what I was told...

There were really only two possible reasons for Madelyn's death:

- She was a "fluke." {God, I hate that word.} Something unexplained happened during her development that caused her issues. Sometimes that happens and the "remedy" would be to "just try again" and hope the same "fluke" didn't show up a second time. Or,
- She had a genetic condition passed to her through her parents. That condition did not allow her to develop properly in the womb and would always be present. The "remedy" would be to "just try again" or have medical intervention—depending on the official medical condition, how much heartbreak we could handle, and what science was capable of.

At first, we were adamant in only knowing Madelyn's medical issues, if those issues were genetic, and what could be done—if anything—to keep this from happening to her future siblings.

If there was a genetic issue, we absolutely, positively did not want to know any more. We did *not* want to know who, if either of us, carried the genetic condition that killed our daughter. Our reason being that we couldn't change genetics— we couldn't change the past—and it would only potentially foster resentment and blame between me and my husband.

Turns out, there were MANY issues, those issues WERE genetic, and medical intervention was the only REAL way to reduce {but not eliminate} the chance of it happening again. The best, and really only, option for giving Madelyn siblings was in vitro fertilization, where the nonviable embryos could be weeded out through pre-implantation testing.

The doctors made it all sound so easy…I didn't have a problem getting or staying pregnant the first time with Madelyn, the embryo was the issue, and science could easily fix that! The *eggs* were just scrambled; the *chicken* wasn't defective. It wasn't until much later in the infertility process did we actually do the math and realize we had a less than six percent chance of having a healthy, happy baby; you get a better score on a school exam just by writing your name!

This is what I had always thought I wanted, and what I had been taught to want growing up: you graduate college, get married, buy a house with a white picket fence and a dog, have babies, grow old, and die. So we dove headfirst into our first of three rounds of IVF, not batting an eye or even thinking about the process or its implications.

——————————— Side Note ———————————

As a 1980s–1990s kid, Mr. Rogers told me growing up if you just try hard enough at anything, you'll eventually get what you want…and I had ALWAYS gotten what I wanted…so why would this be any different? {I mean, I *was* elected mayor of Exchange City in fifth grade by my classmates—my first year at a new school…}

So, we found the "best" doctor money could buy in the Midwest and got to work…

Now it's your turn. You pick where you want to go:

Want to know what happens next? ((Surprise! It's a baby!! —PSYCH. Psych, psych, psych.)) Turn to **page 131** for **Bargaining—My Personal Story.**

Wanna know how to totally piss me off? Just do this one thing and you're on my list, buddy. **Turn the page** for **Kvetching Sphere.**

About now is probably a good time to remind you that **Any Loss Is Grieveable.** It doesn't have to be a dead baby or your house burning down. Turn to **page 45** for the reminder.

KVETCHING SPHERE

---

kvetch [kvech]

verb (used without object): to complain, especially chronically.

noun: Also **kvetch·er.** A person who kvetches.

Have you ever heard of a kvetch? {It's now my new favorite
word, by the way.} Kvetch is originally Yiddish for (basically)
a big fat complainer.

I realized, especially right after Madelyn died, there were
people in my life I couldn't get away from fast enough. People

I previously enjoyed being around but now if I saw them coming I would run the other way {or pretend to be asleep… which, when you're stuck on bed rest, is a more likely option than you'd think}.

I vividly remember sitting in the church basement just minutes after Madelyn's funeral. Even though I wasn't in my right mind, I felt obligated to make the rounds, thank everyone for coming, and to make polite conversation…I needed to feel useful. {I failed miserably, but I think everyone expected the failure and gave me grace.}

A longtime acquaintance came to give me a hug, and as I turned to face her, I saw her belly was the size of a watermelon. Maybe I had known she was pregnant, but to be honest, I couldn't remember if I had put on clothes that day without looking down. After pleasantries were exchanged, she launched into how difficult her pregnancy was and wanted to know every single detail of Madelyn's death:

"What happened?'"
"Do you know what caused it?"
"Could they have caught it earlier?"
"What could have been done to stop it?"
"Is it genetic?"
"Will it happen again?"
"Did you do something wrong?"

I didn't even have the answers to these questions myself. And I don't remember her taking a breath between questions either. I couldn't have answered them if I wanted to. I guess she was mostly concerned with if this would happen to her baby too.

I had another friend who, whenever Madelyn was brought up in conversation {not always by me, I might add—it was usually her}, either started to cry or to rant about how I was not healing properly and needed to "move on." This would either dissolve into my being *her* shoulder to cry on or turn into a knock-down, drag-out fight.

Here I am, already emotionally and physically drained because my daughter is dead, and you want me to console *you* and ease *your* mind? I resent being put in this situation and resent you for putting me there.

Even now, years later, I do my best to stay out of certain people's line of sight. Their presence drains me and their behavior, all those years ago, irks me no end...still...

I feel, especially when it comes to Madelyn, it's all about me. Her world revolves around me. If anyone gets to have an opinion, an emotion, or a reaction, it's me {and Kyle too, I guess}.

Come to find out there's a whole psychological concept around this idea. Originally called "The Ring Theory," it is now more commonly known as the "Kvetching Sphere." Susan Silk first published the article "How Not to Say the Wrong Thing" in the *Los Angeles Times* in 2013[4] based on

4   Silk, Susan and Barry Goldman. "How Not to Say the Wrong Thing." *Los Angeles Times*, 2013.

her experience with others' dealing with her diagnosis of breast cancer.

Here's what she wrote:

"Draw a circle. This is the center ring. In it, put the name of the person at the center of the current trauma. Now draw a larger circle around the first one. In that ring put the name of the person next closest to the trauma. Repeat the process as many times as you need. In each larger ring put the next closest people. Parents and children before more distant relatives. Intimate friends in smaller rings, less intimate friends in larger ones. When you are done you have a Kvetching Order."

The person in the center circle gets to say anything they want *to* any*one* they want. They can whine, complain, curse, and kvetch all the live-long day if they need to. Anyone else involved can do and say all those same things—but only to the people in larger, outer rings. If they are talking to someone in a smaller, inner ring (i.e., closer to the heart of the crisis), the only goal is to help, comfort, and support.

Comfort in, b!tch out.

So, here's what my Kvetching Sphere looks like:

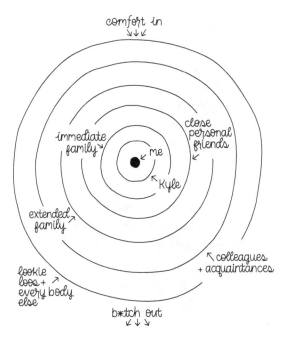

I am the center of this universe. I, and only I, get to behave, talk, whine, kvetch, scream, etc. how I want {but, that doesn't mean I get to be a d!ck}, and hopefully, those around me will comfort me through the crisis.

The schoolmate who was complaining about her pregnancy was "b!tching in." The person who told me to "get over it" was "b!tching in."

THAT is why I still have an aversion to them. I think if I had known at the time WHY I was having the reaction I was to these people, I could have (maybe) controlled the situation (and my reaction) better.

The goal of sharing this concept with you is, if you are in a larger circle, to help you realize what you're saying to whom. Are you comforting or are you b!tching? And, is it having the opposite effect of what you intend?

If you are part of the inner circle, having a name for what you're feeling gives you power and allows you to make choices about your situation {hopefully before it forever taints your relationships with others}.

—————————— Extra Bonus Tip ——————————

This doesn't just apply to those going through a crisis. You can use it for any situation or conversation. If you are constantly kvetching to the inner circle (the person the story/situation/conversation centers around) and making it all about you, you will begin to isolate those people, and they'll quit hanging around. {I know, I've had that happen too; I can give you names.}

Now it's your turn. How do you want to proceed?

Wanna know other things you don't get to do or say to those grieving—but I can do and say? **Turn the page** for **Don't You Call My Husband an @$$hole.**

Think I'm just full of it? Doubting the Kvetching Sphere and its concept? Turn to **page 205** for **When in Doubt, Get More Information.**

Have you gotten yourself all worked up thinking about those who have kvetched inward to you? Maybe now would be a good time to **Just F'ing Breathe.** Turn to **page 69.**

DON'T YOU CALL MY HUSBAND AN @$$HOLE

———

Platitudes are absolute cr@p. There's no two ways around it. The actual definition of platitude {go ahead, look it up—I'll wait} is a trite, meaningless, or prosaic statement, often used as a thought-terminating cliché, aimed at quelling social, emotional, or cognitive unease. {If that doesn't just scream STFU, then nothing does.} Platitudes are used to make the SPEAKER feel better {because they don't know what else to say, they've heard it said before, and it *seems* like a good idea}.

Here's my take on that:

Platitudes are just like calling my husband an @$$hole. You see, I SIGNED UP to be stuck with this guy for the rest of my natural born life. I'm legally and morally obligated to his good, his bad, and his ugly…I know every little thing about him…even the stuff that no human should ever have to know about another human….

- I smile and nod when he says stupid sh!t. {My favorite? "Why do they call $100 bills "Benjamin"? It's Franklin that's printed…oh wait, never mind.}

- I dial 9-1 when he climbs on the roof to put up the Christmas lights and wait to hear the scream followed by the thump before I dial the final 1…
- I keep little treats and snacks in my pocket at all times, so when his blood sugar dips he doesn't get "hangry."

I KNOW when he's being an @$$hole and I GET to call him out on it. That's my privilege as his wife.

You don't. When you call him an @$$hole, I take that personally, and we're gonna rumble. Let's take this out back to the alley.

Same with this platitudes bullsh!t. I get to decide if, and when, those {stupid little} sayings become my silver linings. I get to decide I'm stronger. I get to decide they're "not in pain anymore." Don't you dare try to thrust that onto me.

While platitudes are generally known, said, and accepted as "facts" {they are on the internet everywhere, they *must* be facts}—you don't get to decide when those "facts" become *my* truths.

I'm now a decade or more into my grief journey, and I have just about come to terms with every one of those stupid sayings. I've *found* how to make peace with them. I've *found* the "for a reason" behind my "everything happens" but please, Please, PLEASE don't try to tell me what it is—that's my job, not yours.

Lemme tell you a {not at all exaggerated} tale of my all-time favorite platitude "sighting":

There I was, minding my own beeswax in a local coffee shop trying to get some work done. One of the regulars came in {I knew they were a regular because I'm also a regular—cold brew, light water with room, please}. Apparently, I looked like I wanted to be bothered {you know, massive headphones on with my head down typing away just screams "talk to me"}.

She got my attention and started chatting *at* (not *with*) me, asking me all kinds of personal questions: "Where do you live?" "Are you married?" "What are you working on?"...I was just waiting for the question "How many kids do you have?"...and there it was, like clockwork. Apparently if you are a woman between the age of 22 and 122 you *must* be asked about your children.

Side Note

In these situations I've learned I have to make a split-second character decision on how I feel about this person. If I think I will see this person again and form a meaningful relationship, then I give the awkward, honest answer (potentially starting a pity party). If you bother me and I don't want anything to do with you in the future, I go with the easier (and untruthful) "None." answer. (More on this later.)

I tell her "no kids for us," hoping she will leave it at that.

"You should tooooooooooooooootally have kids. You would make a great mother. My daughter saved my life. You better hurry up though, the clock is ticking, and time isn't slowing down!"

After a good four minutes of her insistent hounding, I look her dead in the eye and say, "I have a daughter, she's dead." In hopes that will make her head spin just enough to get her to quit talking and leave me alone.

She takes a quick beat and gets going again:

"What happened? Have you tried again? Sometimes that just happens. Was she stillborn? How long did she live? What was her name?"

And then, get this, "**At least you never got to know her.**"

Ohhh b!tch! Hold ma hoops! That's it, the end. You're dead to me. Like f'ing hell I didn't get to know her. She lived inside me for thirty-five weeks—and outside of me for eight hours. I have the physical and emotional scars to prove it. She had more of a personality than you ever will. She liked Dr. Seuss and classical remakes of rock songs. She kicked when she heard Daddy's voice. I heard her coo, I saw her beautiful blue eyes.

Okay, I didn't actually SAY any of that out loud to her, but I thought every last word of it while she continued to ramble on (and on and on) about her child and how special she was...

Needless to say, I checked out. She kept talking. I quit listening.

I still see her from time to time, and I try not to murder her with my eyes, but I'm not 100 percent sure it works.

…Oh, and while we're on the subject—here is some other sh!t you don't get to say to me…

- You're never given more than you can handle.
- Everything happens for a reason.
- They're in a better place.
- They wouldn't want you to be sad.
- At least they're not in pain anymore.
- At least…well "at least" followed by literally anything else.
- It's gonna get better.
- God needed them more than you did.
- God wanted it this way.
- God has something better in store for you.
- When one door closes, another door opens.
- Sometimes bad things happen to good people.
- If it doesn't kill you, it makes you stronger.
- Time heals all wounds.
- You need to just get over it.
- Keep calm and carry on.
- You weren't praying, wishing, or hoping hard enough.
- You aren't letting them "Rest in Peace."
- Fake it till you make it.
- It is what it is.
- It could always be worse.
- You need to be strong for others.
- Be grateful for the memories you do have.
- Be thankful for your other children.
- Just keep busy.
- You need to come to terms and accept it.
- You can always have more children.

While this is not an all-encompassing list {I literally have a list longer than a CVS receipt—I've heard them all}, hopefully this is enough to make you realize AND think about the words you use before they come out of your mouth. Even I sometimes, on those very rare occasions, catch myself about to say some of the above phrases to others…but I've learned to stop myself. It's just not helpful, and often more hurtful. {Remember that grief and guilt thing?}

─────────────── Side Note ───────────────

My husband, Kyle, is an absolute saint. Not only does he put up with my cockamamie ideas {I'm going to give up my perfectly good job and start a company from scratch! Let's move to Switzerland! I'm gonna write a book!}, but he is also so helpful, hardly ever whines when I ask for something, and does (more than) his fair share of the household chores. The "a-word" rarely, if ever, is used in our house. It's only when something unforgivable is done—like leaving a wet towel on the bed. My husband IS NOT, in fact, an @$$hole. We both want you to know.

Now it's your turn. Where do you wanna go next?

Wanna know about other cr@p you don't get to do while I'm grieving? **Turn the page for Grief Shaming and Victim Blaming.**

Did I just tick you off with the above list of things you don't get to say? Turn to **page 83** because **This Might Not Be Your Time.**

Or, maybe you need to just **Go Duck Yourself** if you don't like the what I have to say. Turn to **page 197.**

GRIEF SHAMING AND VICTIM BLAMING

———

Here is a very recent {like last week recent} story:

As you can probably imagine, I'm a member of a few online "Loss Mama" support groups. {Okay, a "few" might be an understatement. "Dozens" is more fitting..."tens of dozens" is the most accurate...}

I don't really post my thoughts much in those groups, but I do like to comment on others' posts as a "well-seasoned traveler" that's been around the block a time or two. I think it's sometimes nice to hear the non-sugar coated version of a story from someone who can actually see the light at the end of the tunnel... Just like employees who have manager mentors, Loss Mamas need people who have come before them to help guide the way too. Mostly, I try to just affirm their feelings or give suggestions that have helped me on my own journey. I "kvetch circle" them {comfort in and b!tch out}.

In one of these groups, a woman I don't know asked if it was normal that it was hard for her to be around (and deal with) other people's children. After her only child died, she felt angry with the world and didn't want to be around them.

My exact response? "That's ABSOLUTELY normal. It took me years to get to the point of not getting the urge to slap children just for being within arm's reach of me…"

If you've met me, you know I wouldn't *actually* hurt a fly {Okay, unless the fly hurt me first…or they deserved it} and I have never actually laid a finger on anyone {again, unless they hurt me first or deserved it…}. This lady, another complete stranger, went off on me:

"How dare you! Children are God's special blessings. You are over the edge. A truly sick person for having such thoughts and you need to seek professional help immediately."

OMG Lady!?!?! Didn't your mama ever teach you if you don't have anything nice to say, don't say anything at all?!?! Keep your d@mned mouth shut, or—if you absolutely must—give me a crying frowning face. Do not go off on a tirade.

Obviously, my feathers got ruffled {and the more I thought about it, the more I wanted to peck her eyes out}. Not only was her intention to make me feel bad for my statement but tangentially to make the original question asker feel ashamed for feeling the way she did also. I took a step back, gave her the grace she didn't offer me and let her feel like she had the higher moral ground.

She was grief shaming me…and I almost accepted and succumbed to it—even all these years later. She made me feel bad *for feeling bad*. She tried to rip away the strength I was hoping to provide another human with my vulnerable {and honest} share.

What I think bothered me more than the actual words she wrote was that she herself had lost a child {otherwise she wouldn't have been a part of this "exclusive" group} and went far out of her way to negate both my emotions AND the initial poster's emotions. That's just low-down dirty. It would have taken her far less energy and effort to just keep scrolling, or even give me a thumbs-down and move along.

Yes, I used strong words. Maybe, ever so slightly, stronger than I actually meant {again, I wouldn't hurt a fly!}—that's my prerogative as the storyteller...creative liberties and all. I wanted to make a point. I wanted this poor grieving lady, so early on her grief journey, to know that ALL her feelings are valid and hers to feel.

You cannot guilt someone out of grief {guilt and grief are four-letter words in my book, which I guess means they're four letter words in THIS book}—just like you cannot blame a victim for being at fault of a crime committed against them.

Comments to grievers that start with "At least," "Why don't you," "You should," and "Jesus would want..." are on the same level as:

"They were asking for it."
"She could have said 'No.'"
"She shouldn't have been dressed like that."
"They knew what they were getting into."

If the above statements make your skin crawl, then so should comments about how a griever *should* grieve. You can't control another's actions just like you can't control another's feelings. However, you CAN control what *you* say, *your* actions, and *your* feelings. Do you really feel better for what you said from your high horse? Do you really gotta make that poor griever feel even more sh!tty than they already do?

Now it's your turn. You decide how you'd like to move forward:

I will see your "Jesus would want..." and raise you a "They're in a better place." **Turn the page** for **Bargaining—My Personal Story.**

Wanna b!tch slap that lady as much as I do? We both need to take a second and remember to **Just F'ing Breathe.** Turn to **page 69.**

Maybe some retail therapy will help you feel better. But, you gotta **Stop Suffer Shopping** first. Turn to **page 165.**

BARGAINING

BARGAINING - MY PERSONAL STORY

———

About halfway through the first round of IVF treatment, I woke up in the middle of the night screaming in a panic {think blood curdling, nightmare scene from a horror movie screaming}. *I was the one with the genetic issue. I was the one who killed my daughter.* What kind of woman—what kind of MOTHER—does that to her baby—knowingly or otherwise? What kind of person inflicts that kind of pain— knowingly or otherwise—on the man she vowed to love the rest of her life?

I KNEW it was me, and my issues, that caused my daughter to die. I was shattered. After a heartfelt talk with my husband {remember, we didn't want to know *who* had the issue} and a whole lot of soul searching, we asked the doctor to confirm my suspicion. If I was already choosing to torture myself for killing my daughter whether we had the concrete facts or not, we might as well know for sure.

The doctor confirmed I was right. It was me. I was the one with the genetic condition that killed Madelyn. Then she increased my antidepressant meds.

I, again, fell down that slippery slope of despair.

- My daughter was dead. Because of me.
- The likelihood of having a family was slim to none. Because of me.
- The man I loved was in excruciating emotional pain. Because of me.

W. T. (Actual) FUUUUUUUUUUCK.

...and you thought I was messed up in the head before...

I honestly didn't know how to make this right for those I loved—if there even was a way to make it "right." I clearly was a lost cause...but those around me could go on to lead a normal, happy life despite me. I did this. I caused this. Not them.

I pleaded with Kyle to divorce me. Yeah, yeah, yeah...I know we said "for better or for worse," but this was WORSER than worse. I felt like the parasites stuck to the grass, stuck to the pre-chewed gum, stuck to the mud, stuck to the bottom of your old, nasty shoe. He could go on with his life—find someone who could give him everything he wanted, everything I couldn't give to him.

This was my lot in life. This was my karma from another lifetime coming back around to get me. For some reason, I deserved this. Kyle did not. I met with an attorney to draw up the paperwork; at least *this* would be easy...we didn't have a whole lot of stuff and no kids to fight over custody for, unless you considered Madelyn's urn.

I know Kyle knew I was serious, but I don't know that he ever really knew how far I had gone toward the actual divorce. {I guess he'll know now...}

There was one day about six months after my genetics revelation, Kyle had to sit me down and set me straight—a "come to Jesus," if you will. He would not, under any circumstances, be signing any papers. He told me he married me—not the family I could or could not give him. Not the possibility of "happily ever after." He married me—for the person I am.

And that was pretty much the end of the discussion. Except occasionally, when it comes up, as a joke, like "You had your chance, buddy. You're stuck with me now."

Now it's your turn. You decide where to go:

I haven't really talked much about Kyle. Maybe you should meet. Wanna know more about him? Turn to **page 117** for **Don't You Call My Husband an @$$hole.**

Don't have psychic powers and wanna read what happens next? Or, maybe you're just a glutton for schadenfreude. Turn to **page 153** for **Depression—My Personal Story.**

Or, just **turn the page** to learn why **You Will Second-Guess** everything you've ever thought.

YOU WILL SECOND-GUESS

———

As you grieve, you will second-guess. You will second-guess everything. You will rehash {and rehash and rehash} every little thing and decision that was made. You might even rethink every single decision you've ever made in your whole life. "What ifs" and "Should haves" will abound as you try to make sense of your all-new, unfamiliar, upside-down world.

Not only did I second-guess {and often belittle} myself for every decision I made throughout my pregnancy:

- There is STILL caffeine {and tons of chemicals} in the one caffeine-free Diet Coke I allowed myself a week.
- Maybe I shouldn't have eaten all that canned soup… did some of the chemicals in the metal can leach into the food? …and I microwaved it in a plastic bowl that probably wasn't completely BPA free…
- Did the laptop end up on my belly too many times? …but I was so cold, and it was so warm!
- My doctor said it was okay if I dyed my hair a couple times while pregnant…didn't she? Oh cr@p, what if she didn't say I could but I did it anyway!!??!!

And shortly after Madelyn died, I had a million "should haves":

- I should have refused the morphine while Madelyn was still alive. I was passed out cold for her entire life.
- Should we have tried to do something to extend her life, so we had more time with her? Maybe we could have removed some of the fluid from her brain...but would I have been able to be any more coherent to be with her? Would prolonging the inevitable have given us any more closure or just caused more pain?
- Should we have pushed the doctors to give us more time with Madelyn in the womb? We just accepted what they said as fact and immediately went in for a C-section when they said to.
- Should I have forced the hospital to give Madelyn pain medication? (They said she wasn't in any pain, but how do we know that for sure?) Or keep me another night... maybe my incision wouldn't have opened up and become infected if I had stayed?
- Should I have spent more time looking into donating her organs to other babies? And why didn't I think about donating my breast milk {maybe my weight wouldn't have ballooned if I had}?
- Why didn't I look at her fingers and toes more closely, snip a lock of her hair, give her more kisses, sing to her...?

Once the cause of Madelyn's death came in, I had a whole new round of "second guessing":

- If I can't have healthy, living children, then why be married at all? It's not fair to bring this wonderful, caring man down with me. Should I ask for the divorce, or should I just surprise him with it?

- If I can't get pregnant, then why was I such a good, studious girl in college? I should have been partying hard and slutting it up!
- Why the hell am I working so hard!?!?! Pinching pennies and saving every extra dime for my imaginary kids and their nonexistent future. Let's go shopping! YOLO!
- And my personal favorite, and the question I'm not sure will ever have an answer: Do I really even want kids? Or, has society trained me to feel inadequate and less than human without tiny humans to take care of? {That debate is another story for another day...I have LOTS of thoughts on that.}

I bring up all my should haves and would haves and what ifs {Okay, not all of them—we don't have enough time, or enough paper in the world} to show that I've literally thought all the thoughts. I've asked myself the logical questions. I've asked myself the illogical questions. I've asked myself the dark and scary questions. You will ask yourself all the same questions. It's okay. Ask yourself those questions.

Once you've asked yourself all the questions and berated yourself for the answers/decisions you made, I want you to remember something: you did the absolute best you could with the information and resources you had at the time.

That statement is so important that I want you to repeat it after me:

I DID THE ABSOLUTE BEST I COULD WITH THE INFORMATION AND RESOURCES I HAD AVAILABLE TO ME AT THE TIME.

Now it's your turn. How do you wanna proceed?

I have five little words for you: **Grief Is Not a Problem**! **Turn the page** and quit treating it like one.

Maybe, after you ask yourself all the questions, you need a reminder to give yourself self-compassion. Turn to **page 51** for **Permission** to do just that.

Or, this was a pretty heavy story. Maybe you need to **Just F'ing Breathe.** Turn to **page 69.**

GRIEF IS NOT A PROBLEM

Here's the thing: grief, like love, is not a problem to be solved. When others try to explain it like it is, it makes me think of the song from *The Sound of Music*: "How do you solve a problem like Maria? How do you catch a cloud and pin it down?"

Um, you don't. That's how. Grief cannot be "solved"; it has to be felt. It has to be experienced. It has to be worked through. If grief were a problem, then it would have an answer, and a RIGHT answer at that. If there were a cure for grief, do you think there would still be people suffering from it? NO! We "answered" polio and now no one suffers from that anymore.

People LOVE to solve problems, especially when those problems involve human suffering, and they love to prove they solved the problem by showing others the solution. Scientists and researchers have been fighting each other for years to be the first to "solve" cancer...and that "only" affects 39 percent of Americans. (Grief affects 100 percent of Americans: Benny Franklin said, "In this world nothing can be said to be certain, except death and taxes." I would argue grief is more prolific than just about anything else based on that quote.) You gotta assume that if someone were actually to solve grief, the answer would be immediately shouted from the mountaintops!

A "grief problem" makes it sound like it's a pressing matter that needs immediate attention and a finite solution. Um, again, don't you think if I had that solution—if a finite answer could even be had—I would be bottling that sh!t up and giving it to anyone who would take it?!?!?!

Because grief is not a problem, we need to quit treating it like it is. Period. The end. Quit trying to hurry up and solve it, hide it, or brush it under the rug...

You experience grief like you experience a museum. I don't know about you, but I can only take so much "museum-ing" at a time {yes, even the Louvre}. I "like" to go and *be* there, amongst the art...see the pieces and experience the space, and then—like that—I'm done. I've had enough "high society" for a while and wanna go back to flip-flops, mullets, and reality TV.

You need to allow yourself to do the same with your grief. Befriend it like your crazy sister-in-law {a little bit goes a long way}. Experience it. Sit with it. Feel your feels, think your thoughts. (If you're smart you might even write some of them down...) Then, take a break.

When it's time (because you decided it was time or the universe told you it was time; *not* because someone else told you), you can go back to the "grief museum" and experience a little more "culture."

There is something to be said for INTENTIONALLY leaving the "grief museum" for something lowbrow: a slapstick comedy, a game of kickball, TMZ, a boardgame, a long bath, or just a sit on the sofa staring at the wall. Just because the museum is ginormous doesn't mean you have to stay there until you see the whole d@mned thing in one fell swoop. And, let's be honest, like anything, at some point you will begin to tune out, glaze over, and walk right past the important stuff. You NEED some time away.

──────────────── Side Note ────────────────

This does not mean you should eat/drink/smoke/snort/shoot your feelings away. That's not a coping mechanism, that's the start to an addiction. Please allow yourself (and others) the opportunity to recognize these behaviors and make the necessary course corrections.

───

Now it's your turn. You decide where to go next:

Still think grief is a problem that can be solved? Turn to **page 55** as a reminder that **There Is No Right Way to Grieve.**

Wanna know who's got it worse with their grief? Well, **My Grief Can Beat Up Your Grief—turn the page** to find out why.

Let's also talk about the difference between **Not Wanting to Be Alive** vs. Wanting to Be Dead. There is a subtle yet very important distinction. Turn to **page 171** to read on.

MY GRIEF CAN BEAT UP YOUR GRIEF

Sometimes I really detest how my mind works. {And I'll bet you a penny your mind works the same way mine does...} My mind is constantly in competition with my "opponents"—real and imaginary. My mind wants to "binary code" everything into a strict scoring metric, so then the world can know who "wins"...at grief and at life in general. I hear others' stories of grief and I impulsively (and unconsciously) start "grading" and comparing mine against theirs. Creating a pluses and deltas list—a kind of masochistic T-chart—remember, I'm a trained accountant. I really think that's just human nature:

- "Well, at least I didn't have to _____." {Again, that f*ing "at least" phrase.}
- "I DID have to _____."
- "My story is different because _____."
- "They *only* had to _____."
- "They *got* to _____."

We *try* to make our grief unique. One of a kind, "better" than everyone else's for the sake of being "qualified" to feel the way we do. {I'm a member of the Xennial generation where we are all "special little snowflakes," so *everything* I do has to be the best and one of a kind...even my sorrow.}

::NEWS FLASH::

Grief is relative to your circumstances and **can't be compared.** {Remember the story I told about my blue Toyotas in Any Loss Is Grieveable?} Knock it off!! Quit trying to!! You're getting a divorce and your friend's mother just died from cancer. Which is worse? Who wins? You both lost relationships you will never get back...

If your beloved cat, Fluffy, dies and that is the worst grief you know, it's not fair for me to say your pain isn't valid because it is not the same as my house burning to the ground.

There is no race to win, no one gets a first place trophy; we all just get crappy participation ribbons. Allow your grief to be uniquely yours AND do not overlook the similarities. Similarities are the nuggets that help you find your "tribe." Those similarities start to allow you to heal your soul. It's the differences (implied or otherwise) that rip us apart and keep us from finding our "new happy." {This also applies to politics, religion, favorite movies, and the best kind of barbecue (Of course it's Kansas City!).}

When I was in the depths of my grief, I found I would put myself into terrible emotional situations {and I was already in a really bad place}. I would find other mamas who lost babies and critique their story to negate their pain {because, for some reason, by negating their pain it would condone my own}:

- They *only* had a miscarriage.
- *At least* (ugh! "at least" again!!) they had their baby for five years.
- They knew from the beginning it wasn't a "viable pregnancy."
- Well, if they had just been better parents...

Looking back, I'm so mad at myself for having these thoughts. Every one of those statements is absolute sh!t. If I would have said them out loud to the other mama, I would have expected her to burn me at the stake. Also, in that specific moment, at that exact time, I had to have those thoughts. It was my version of coping.

It is *reasonable* to think these thoughts and try to make these comparisons—initially. I think we all do it in the heat of the moment (most of the time subconsciously). That does not make it healthy. That doesn't make it right. The sooner you can recognize that you are suffering from "comparison-itis" (the disease of comparing) and knock that sh!t off, the sooner your "new happy" will become a reality.

I'd like to pose a question: Can we just realize we're all suffering in our own unique prison and support each other? Let's quit comparing and start connecting. Let's talk about all the similarities of our personal hells; I promise there are some. Finding those similarities and latching onto them like the floating door in *Titanic* might just save our lives.

Now it's your turn. Where do you want to go?

Shall we play a game? ::*said* War Games *style::* *How about Global Thermonuclear War?* Later? Okay. Let's play **Two Truths {and A Lie}.** Turn to **page 193.** {Or maybe you'd prefer a good game of chess?}

Just knock it off! Turn to **page 165** to **Stop Suffer Shopping**. It's not what you think, and it's not as fabulous as you'd hoped.

"Comparison-itis," Suffer Shopping, and **Grief Ghettos**— OH MY! We might as well finish out that trifecta. Turn to **page 159** to see if you're living in the grief ghetto.

Or, let's look for a positive spin on this beast! {You know, we should really do that some- times...} **Turn the page** to **Do More Good Sh!t.**

DO MORE GOOD SH!T

You'll start to learn along your grief journey what makes you feel less bad. {Let's be honest, things won't make you feel good…they'll just make you feel less bad.} Maybe it's reading, maybe it's talking to friends, watching movies, going on a walk, playing board games, volunteering, or learning something new.

As you start to find little {or big!} things that make you feel less bad, start doing more of those things. And make a list of those things for when you're having one of those "ebbing" times and you're feeling "badder." Then, you can look at your list and find something that will make you feel "less bad."

Taking those baby steps toward feeling less bad will begin to add up over time. Someday, hopefully, your less bad will become better, and then better will become good {and gooder, and gooder}.

Early on especially, I found I had a hard time sitting still; my mind was constantly racing {but not so much I could actually use my mind in a meaningful way}. My grief not only stole my mind, it also stole my energy. The good sh!t I found to do was with my hands (it didn't take much energy or brain power, but it did do good for myself and for others).

I began crocheting {yes, I'm actually 108 years old} octopuses for the organization Octopus for a Preemie. I made several, then realized I was terrible at it and couldn't comply with the rules and regulations enough to actually be able to donate the Amigurumi to hospital NICU departments. Maybe it was because I wasn't skilled enough at crocheting; maybe I didn't have the patience; maybe the pattern was too complicated for this newbie, or I didn't have the right tools. I don't know. I just couldn't get it together enough to create an acceptable end product. I found the good sh!t I was doing was actually making me feel sh!ttier than if I had done no sh!t at all. So I quit. I didn't need another reminder I wasn't good enough.

But, in the process of learning to crochet, I found it was therapeutic. I liked that it could be done in tandem while watching something mindless on TV {maybe the wavy static of a dead channel?}. It didn't *really* require much skill and brain power, but it was just tough enough to start and stop that I couldn't also be shoving my face full of Oreo cookies at the same time. Plus, as an added bonus there was a very low likelihood of impaling myself with the with crochet hook {something my knitting needles seemed to do frequently—I told you, I'm an old soul}.

So, I found another organization I could donate my crafting time to—this time baby blankets! {Much fewer guidelines and restrictions}. This was perfect…or was it? I loved to start a new blanket but would find I would get bored. I'd put it down partway through and never pick it back up. I needed instant gratification.

Enter "Project Robby" (projectrobby.com). This local Kansas organization gives care packages to loss families all over the country which include teeny-tiny crocheted angel wings. That was totally my speed: easy pattern, few {if any} restrictions, and if I really get going I can knock out a few sets in an evening! ...not to mention the solace that the loss families got by receiving the wings...

I certainly go through spurts of doing my "good sh!t." Sometimes I'll go through an entire skein of yarn in a weekend; other times I'll have to turn the house upside down trying to remember where I put my supplies. I'm not consistent with my "good sh!t," but when I'm able, I get my fix, and it really lifts my spirits.

Other "fixes" come and go from my repertoire (iron-ruining perler beads, sewing, Legos, scrapbooking, puzzles, coloring, running...), but this (crocheting baby angel wings) seems to be my staple and always helps me feel good when I'm down.

Find something, *anything,* that lifts your spirits and brings a smile to your face, even if it's just a little one, and keep that in the back of your mind for your gloomy days. If your "sh!t" requires supplies, keep a small stash around so it's not a barrier to your good vibes {craft supplies *always* seem to be 50 percent off at craft stores}. Find "sh!t" that you can do solo and with others {again, don't let needing a buddy keep you from your happy juju}.

Your list of "good sh!t" can, and will, change, adjust, and shift over time too. Take things off your list which don't give you the same feeling they once did. Add new things to your list as you find them. Just knowing you have this list somewhere of "happiness-inducing activities" is sometimes all you need for a boost.

Now it's your turn. You decide how you'd like to move forward:

Ready to add another car to the "Good Sh!t Express?"
Turn to **page 185** to **Write It Down and Work It Out, B!tch**.

Think this "good sh!t" isn't enough to make a meaning-ful difference? I got something else for you that might help: **You'll Set Yourself Free** by turning to **page 223.**

Or, are you feeling a little too good about yourself? Let's get depressed. **Turn the page** for **Depression—My Personal Story.**

DEPRESSION - MY
PERSONAL STORY

———

Just because Kyle had forgiven me for all the terrible things I had done to him {unknowingly—I promise}, I hadn't forgiven myself. I went even deeper down the "grief hole" than ever before. I, single-handedly, caused so much pain and suffering for so many. I went back into the "if everything happens for a reason" bullsh!t bubble...and stayed there for a very long time...

I killed my daughter. Because Madelyn died and needed someone to care for her, Kent and Jane were killed. Therefore, I killed Kent and Jane and caused so much pain and sorrow to everyone I love.

Yeah, that's exactly where my mind went.

BUT {that's a big, Big, BIG but} if I could bring Madelyn siblings, I might *begin* to right some of the wrongs I had caused. It was really the only thing I felt I could do to make it "right." (I'm not saying it made any logical sense, but how else do you start to make a situation like this "right" again?) So, I threw myself into the IVF process. I ate, slept, and breathed bringing living babies into the world. I consumed all the right foods, took all the pills and supplements {even the ones that tasted like, and made me, puke}, I started acupuncture even though I don't really care for needles. You name it, I became a disciple of the practice.

Everyone was hopeful and optimistic {especially the doctors who were taking my money}. At least 75 percent of my eggs were "scrambled," so we were convinced it was *just* a numbers game. Getting more eggs = better chance of a healthy baby. The doctors filled me to the brim with medication to get the most eggs possible—to the point my ovaries were the size of grapefruits. {For reference that's about five to ten times larger than normal. Think you're uncomfortable and feel bloated after a big meal? Double that, then double that, then feel that way for three weeks straight.}

My levels were monitored and reported as "great." My counts were done and reported as "awesome." I was even told more than once I had a "rock star uterus" {I'm thinking about adding that to my resume...}

Then retrieval day came, and science took over. I had done all I could, now we waited...twenty-seven eggs led to fourteen fertilizing (great), led to seven growing to day three (good), led to four getting to day five testing (still good), led to none (ZERO, Nada, ZILCH) testing normal and being able to implant (...heart shattered...).

We did this same IVF process two more times in two states with three doctors over the course of four years. Each time with the same roller coaster outcome: awesome, great, great, could be better, great, great, good, sucks to be you. There was even a time we drove our little embryo baby family the nine hours to Chicago for special testing hoping it would bring us more favorable results. {When you counted Kyle, me, Madelyn's urn and pink stuffed turtle, and our fifteen embryo babies in the electric cooler in the back seat we teased that our Prius was actually a clown car—easily holding nineteen passengers PLUS luggage!}

It was on the way home from that trip we got the call saying none of our "babies" would survive. We had to pull the car over on the side of the interstate for about an hour until we could see past the tears enough to begin driving again.

We went from "it's just a numbers game; a matter of time" to the only biological child we have lives in an urn on the nightstand next to my alarm clock (in what felt like) overnight.

My life was on pause for almost five years {wavy VHS pause lines included}—the entire time we were trying to grow our family. After the fact, I realized I was afraid to make any decisions that could affect our future nonexistent family in any way. I couldn't mentally move forward until I was able to prove to the universe, and myself, I was a worthy woman, wife, and mother. I thought {and was raised to believe} motherhood equaled happiness.

I was devastated when it didn't pan out, when I couldn't "control and conquer" the life I thought I desired into existence. And, worst of all, I didn't have anyone to talk to who truly understood what I was going through and the universe-altering questions I was asking myself. {Kyle, obviously, was a very close runner up—he just didn't have all the right body parts to fully understand.}

I realized, once we had finally decided we needed to be done with IVF, I just continued to compound and complicate my cumulative grief by never processing one event before trying to "prove the universe wrong" with the next. It was time for me to take time for me. I needed to unpack that nasty, ugly, worn out luggage I'd been carrying, and sort some things out.

I needed to pause from my already paused life to reflect on all that had happened, try to get my head back on straight, detox from all the drugs, hormones, pills, and supplements I'd been pumped full of...and work toward becoming the person I was supposed to be.

I'm not sure anyone can truly understand the toll {emotionally, physically, spiritually, and every other kind of "ly" there is} that infertility and treatments take on a person, and a couple. {Unless, of course, you've lived through that "Hell on Earth" yourself.} You squeeze an entire lifetime of emotions into the teeny-tiny span of just a few months. The excitement and anticipation of a new life. The rocky road, and ups and downs, of that life; then the devastation and despair of the death—of your dream child (that to everyone but you never existed), and, ultimately, the life you hoped to have had.

After hundreds of hours of medical treatments, tens of thousands of dollars, and a pause on life for the last five years, it felt like this was really the end of the story. This was the end of it all. Now what? What is the purpose of life? Why do I even exist?

If I read one more sob story that ends with "then we had a baby and I found meaning and purpose in life again," I will definitely sucker punch someone.

Why does THAT have to be the "be all, end all" to the story? Why is THAT the happy ending that makes everything... well—happy?

That cr@p on a cracker story is making all us barren and childless women feel less than human.

Last I checked, the only thing that can make a person happy is themselves. Let's quit proliferating this ridiculous notion that bringing other tiny humans into existence fixes all our sorrow.

Can we just stop and think that maybe, just maybe, having children isn't all it's cracked up to be? That we can provide goodness and value in the world without bringing munchkins into it? {Have you ever thought society HAS to convince itself having babies will "make everything right in the world," otherwise mankind will cease to exist?}

_____

It took a long freaking-fracking time to realize my life's purpose {seeing as my societal-issued purpose was now null and void}...

...until I finally did realize my purpose, I curled up in my self-dug hole and had a pity party—for all the things I DIDN'T have in my life...

Now it's your turn. You decide where to go next:

Want to know how I started feeling un-sorry for myself? It was simple. It wasn't easy. Turn to **page 179** for **Testing—My Personal Story.**

Maybe you just wanna keep hating life and everything in it. **Turn the page** to learn all about the mind, body, and time suck that is the **Grief Ghetto.**

ESPECIALLY when you're in the pit of depression you need a reminder: **Don't Believe The Things You Tell Yourself...** Turn to **page 59.**

GRIEF GHETTO

———

Personally, I've always been a little bit leery of support groups. Honestly, I don't know why—just something about them gives me the heebie-jeebies. In-person groups: they're okay, I guess– but really I've had my eye on online support groups. I think they can be double-edged swords. And if the group isn't properly monitored and maintained, then it can become a big ol' mess of smarmy sewage.

Online support groups are especially susceptible to trolls, bad actors, and individuals who are "stuck" in their grief because of the unique component of anonymity—something you really only get online. Members can "hide" behind made-up usernames, fake profile pictures, and misleading information. It's a little bit harder to "catfish" in real life, which is why in-person groups rank a little higher on my list.

On the pro side of the support group coin is the community. {I mean come on, that's what Sharing Solace is almost exclusively about: the community aspect.} Inside these groups you're surrounded by people who have "been there and done that." They understand what you're going through, which helps you to feel less crazy as you process your own emotions and thoughts.

The members can give each other advice and tips which have helped them traverse their own rocky terrain and can provide support and guidance. More than anything {I'm going to say it again because I think it's SO important}, the other members of the group can help you feel less crazy about your "nonsensical" thoughts and feelings. There is just something about getting those tidbits of information from someone who's been in the trenches—not just read about what it's like to be in the trenches.

On the con side of that same coin is the idea of the "crab complex." When crabs are dumped in a bucket, they pull each other back to the bottom as they all try to move themselves upward. They're not specifically trying to keep the other crabs down; they're just trying to get themselves to higher altitude.

This concept also fits with some members of a support group. (IMHO) If the group is not overseen with a "healthy" direction, the group can degrade into a "big d!ck" contest...or a "My Grief Can Beat Up Your Grief" expo. It's not that the members are intentionally trying to compare and pull others back down to the bottom of the grief bucket: they're just trying to make themselves feel a little better...oftentimes at the expense of others... {remember the story in Grief Shaming and Victim Blaming?}

The term "Grief Ghetto" was found in a 2017 Swedish study by Dorthe Refslund Christensen, Ylva Hård af Segerstad, Dick Kasperowski and Kjetil Sandvik {...Don't worry, I can't pronounce their names either...} While it's not known if the phrase "Grief Ghetto" was intended by the researchers or was created in translation, I think it's absolutely fitting! The traumatically bereaved is definitely a "restricted, isolated, and segregated group."

This study titled "Bereaved Parents' Online Grief Communities: De-Tabooing Practices or Relation-Building Grief-Ghettos?"[5] concludes:

"We observe that the online forums take on the shape of grief ghettos, which exhibit positive qualities: the forums are safe havens for the bereaved parents' grief work and continuing bonds practices. On the other hand, the ghetto may also function as a place for inventing new restrictive norms for how these practices may be shaped and expressed."

There you go! Even the research shows you have to take support groups with a grain of salt. Support groups, online or IRL, can have both positive and negative effects on the griever. Those effects need to be weighed from time to time to determine if a group is still the best method of support. {And only the griever can make this determination for themselves.}

If you, yourself, are contemplating finding a support group, I still highly recommend it, with a little word of caution. It's okay to go "support shopping" {it's NOT okay to go suffer shopping…see the next chapter}. Explore different types of groups. Maybe that means different meeting formats, different types of attendees, different areas of your city…keep "shopping" until you find a group that suits your present

---

5   "Bereaved Parents' Online Grief Communities: De-Tabooing Practices or Relation-Building Grief-Ghettos?" *Journal of Broadcasting & Electronic Media*, 2020.

needs and has a similar thought process as your own—don't *just* join a group because it's the most convenient.

And also, don't guilt yourself into believing you NEED a support group; not everyone does. If a support group is not right for you, that's completely fine. Do not force yourself into becoming a "support groupie." A 2016 study titled "The Effect of Bereavement Groups on Grief, Anxiety, and Depression—A Controlled, Prospective Intervention Study"[6] by Ulla Näppä, Ann-Britt Lundgren, and Bertil Axelsson found that grievers who *chose* not to participate in support groups were actually found to report *lower* levels of grief after one year:

"Participation in bereavement groups did not produce any effects on grief, anxiety, or depression in comparison to non-participants who were unable to participate. Non-participants who did not want to participate reported lower levels of grief and anxiety than the other two groups."

This implies that if you force yourself into a support group (online or otherwise), when you don't think it is the right fit for you, you can actually be doing yourself more damage than you thought. I find this fascinating. The first question I almost always got after telling others my daughter died {after the required "How did it happen?/How long did she live?" rigmarole} was: "Are you part of a support group?"

6   Näppä, Ulla, Ann-Britt Lundgren, and Bertil Axelsson. "The Effect Of Bereavement Groups On Grief, Anxiety, And Depression—A Controlled, Prospective Intervention Study." *BMC Palliative Care* 15 (1), 2016. doi:10.1186/s12904-016-0129-0.

If a support group feels good in your heart, then go for it! Find a group that "fills your tank" and you enjoy being a part of. If support groups aren't your bag, no worries. The research shows if you want to participate but are unable to, you're not causing yourself harm.

If a support group doesn't interest you then don't force it; again, the study shows that forcing attendance actually causes more psychological damage.

What is this telling us? Say it with me: There Is No Right Way to Grieve.

There are so many other options out there to explore your feelings: art, music, talk, group, individual, play. Don't guilt yourself into (or out of) your grief or how you choose to support it. Do what feels right for you, and don't let others tell you it's wrong.

Now it's your turn. You pick where you wanna go:

Now you know it's okay to go support shopping, but you have to **Stop Suffer Shopping. Turn the page** to learn more.

Or maybe you need to remember **You'll Set Yourself Free**, if you choose to? Turn to **page 223.**

Need a refresher of **Grief Shaming and Victim Blaming** from above? Flip to **page 125.**

STOP SUFFER SHOPPING

———

Haruki Murakami (reread that, I did not write "Hakuna Matata"…and now you'll be singing it all day…) said, "Pain is inevitable. Suffering is optional." This quote from *What I Talk About When I Talk About Running* is actually about {you guessed it} running. And it goes on: "Say you're running, and you think, 'Man, this hurts, I can't take it anymore.' The 'hurt' part is an unavoidable reality, but whether you can stand anymore is up to the runner himself."

Pain is going to happen in your life: physical pain, emotional pain, mental pain, spiritual pain—it will all happen. Pain comes to you in the present moment. You prick your finger, that is current pain. If you think about that finger prick and how it's going to hinder you from being able to type your dissertation over the next few days…and what are you going to do…and if you don't get this paper done, you'll never get your degree…then you'll never get a job…and you'll have to become a bag lady living in a van down by the river…that's unnecessary suffering.

The pain of the finger prick is going to happen {you need to have blood drawn}. The suffering of how the finger prick will affect your life in the future is completely up to you. You can allow your worrying to cause you suffering from the pain;

or you can experience the pain, FEEL the pain, and then move forward.

Pain comes to you in the present. Projecting the pain into the future or onto the past is suffering.

When Madelyn died in my arms in 2010, that was pain—excruciating pain. That was the worst pain I'd ever felt in my entire life. I took that pain and projected it into the future: thinking about all the things I wouldn't get to do because she had died. And projected it into the past: what did I do wrong during the pregnancy that caused her to die? That was (un)necessary suffering.

One of the best ways I've found to "help" reduce suffering from thinking about the past is to just try to get answers. I had hundreds of "could it have beens" floating around in my mind: Was it my hair dye? Did I have too much caffeine? Too much sugar? Did I rest the laptop on my belly one too many times? Did I not eat enough vegetables? Too many carbs? Should I have gone to the gym more? Less? Was I "too sad" my aunt and uncle died?…or maybe I wasn't sad enough… There was absolutely nothing I could have done to save my Maddie's life—but the only way to know that was to ask the questions and get the answers.

The thing about answers is, no matter what, you're probably not going to like them. The answers from the past are not going to change the present. If the doctor had told me I could have saved Madelyn by just doing _____, I would have been both relieved in knowing the answer and even madder at myself because I *actually* caused her death {opposed to the "made up actually" because I have wonky genetics}. Once you have those answers to your questions, you can begin to process the coulda/woulda/shouldas in your life.

I've found there is only so much you can do to stop future suffering. If you let it, it will eat you alive {I know, I almost let it}. As you experience "future suffering," I find it's best to get it out of your head and onto the page. By writing it down, it helps to keep you from "stewing" about it—like that finger prick. (See Write It Down and Work It Out, B!tch on page 185.) The more you stew about this being the first Thanksgiving without your loved one, the more mountainous the suffering will become.

You need to allow yourself to feel your emotions but not go overboard. Writing it down allows you to put words to your feelings {it's not always as easy as it sounds}, and also have those words for posterity. When Christmas rolls around and you begin to have the same feeling, you are able to go back to your written words, reread them, and amend them as you need.

Here's another analogy: your partner breaks up with you {divorce, breakup, friendship goes kaput, company dissolves, it really doesn't much matter what type of breakup it is}. There is present pain in that breakup; it hurts to end any type of relationship.

The suffering comes by going through the past with a fine-tooth comb trying to see where you could have changed something, where something could have been "fixed" (what's done is done) or stalking them on social media to see what they're up to now, if they seem like they miss you, and if they've already moved on {that's just pouring salt in your open wound}.

Instead, realize your current pain has changed your dreams, plans, and control of the future—abruptly. Acknowledge that. Feel that. Explore your current pain. How does your "new present" change what you thought about the future? Now, allow your present pain to be intermixed with present pleasure: talk to a friend about nothing in particular, go see a movie, take a bubble bath, paint, read...

Pain needs to be felt and supported {that's why nurses give you the really good drugs after surgery}. Suffering needs to be adjusted {But they don't give you those drugs forever, do they?}.

Don't shop for unneeded suffering by projecting your pain into the past or future.

Life can make you bitter. Or it can make you better. You can choose to be bitter by staying frozen and trying to "fix" the past and control the future. Or, you can choose to become better by living in the "new present" and accepting the loss of the future you created in your mind. I challenge you to choose to be better.

Now it's your turn. You decide how you'd like to move forward:

Still feel like you wanna do some more suffer shopping? **Turn the page** to explore **Not Wanting to Be Alive.**

Need a break from your suffer shopping? Throw caution to the wind! Turn to **page 231** 'cause **Hey Baby, Let's Go to Vegas!**

Or, maybe you need a reminder it's okay to feel your feels. Turn back to **page 51.** I grant you that **Permission.**

Like the idea of getting answers to your questions? **When in Doubt, Get More Information** by going to **page 205.**

NOT WANTING TO BE ALIVE

Let's not sugarcoat this: not wanting to be alive is grief. Wanting to be dead is suicidal. There is a difference. Very simply, one is normal, and the other needs medical attention. {The phone number for the National Suicide Prevention Lifeline is 1-800-273-8255. Use it.}

There are many times I want to be with my daughter. Since I can't bring her back {believe me, I've tried willing that into existence so much that if anyone could pull it off, it would be me}; the only other option is to meet her where she is. I had that feeling a LOT early on, and it continues to taper off the longer I survive past her death. Now, more often than not, I realize I need to stay here on Earth to honor her memory by being a good human and through my work with Sharing Solace.

Not wanting to be alive is grief; that is a normal part of the healing process. You believe the emotional pain is so unbearable and there is only one way to "make it go away." It does not mean you are crazy. You should not be locked up. YOU. ARE. NORMAL.

Wanting to be dead is…let's just say…less healthy. Wanting to be dead means you've thought through a plan, or you might have started making changes to your life to facilitate the "act." I say this out of love and support. Please reach out to someone you trust and can confide in: a friend or family member, a neighbor, a licensed professional, a grief sherpa… Seek counseling. Meet with your doctor. Find a mentor.

Do not be the HERO and try to "just power through." You are not "less of a person" because you want and/or need intervention. Medication is an acceptable proactive remedy. {You know I'm on "happy pills"; I'm not going to hide it.}

Even being acutely aware of the subtle differences, I am constantly walking that fine line myself. And, I want you to know it's okay—just please, please, please, please seek out the assistance you need when you feel you're veering toward the dark side. {Luke, I am not your father, but I still want the best for you.}

Here's how I "know" when I'm getting a little too dark for my comfort {in the hope it might help you to recognize similar actions in your own life}. I find, when I'm headed down that "little too goth/emo" path {yes, I understand the difference—I'm a child of both generations and can identify as and with both}, I start doing stupid things in my car when I'm alone. I don't put on my seat belt; I text when I know I shouldn't; I "make it through that pink light," and I speed more than I normally allow myself to speed {the speed limit is still for nerds!}.

The seat belt one is the biggie for me. Luckily, my car is smarter than its driver and beeps like it's gonna explode for about five minutes or until the driver puts it on. Sometimes it honestly just slips my mind and the beeping reminds me. I know I'm headed down that slippery slope when I hear the beep and just crank the tunes {another one of my "goth/emo" stupid things} to drown out the beeping noise until it stops.

Sometimes it takes me a time or two to realize I'm being an idiot…but when I do realize, I do my little self-assessment:

- Am I taking my antidepressant as I'm supposed to…or have I "forgotten" lately?
- Am I practicing self-care *and* self-compassion?
- When was the last time I saw my counselor?
- Have I gotten in my physical activity for the week?
- Have I seen people who feed my soul lately?
- Have I seen too many of the people who "drain my tank"?
- Have a left my house and seen the sun in the last forty-eight hours?
- Have a allowed myself to feel my feelings?

More often than not, it's "just" one of the above things being catawampus. I make note, make adjustments, and course correct. If all my pieces are in alignment, I know I need to dig a little deeper; normally, that's an extra chat with my therapist and/or mentor.

——————— Speaking of Professional Support ———————

We all go {or at least should go} to the doctor regularly for checkups. Get our blood sugar checked and our resting heart rate… Why isn't it more socially acceptable to go to a mental health professional for a "checkup from the neck up"? (Zig Ziglar said that.) Maybe if we talked about it a little more, it would become more socially acceptable. So here it goes. "Hi.

I'm Crystal and I see a therapist regularly." {{Group chant: "Hi, Crystal."}}

If you need help finding a therapist in your area, please visit www.psychologytoday.com. If you want help with a grief mentor come to www.SharingSolace.com.

Every once in a blue moon, it's more than "just" an extra chat with my lady; medications need to be adjusted or changed. I need to have a long talk with myself or others. I have to let go of something (a feeling, stress, a project, whatever it is...).

The key, I've found, is to be able to see and recognize those "little" changes in my behavior before they become BIG behaviors (and are harder to adjust and come back from). Many little baby adjustments over an extended period of time are much easier to make than one big @$$ adjustment in one fell swoop...

Maybe erratic driving isn't your thing. It could be food, or sleep schedule, or work habits. Whatever it is, if you can become self-aware enough to pinpoint it and make note of your routine changes, you'll be much further ahead of most people. And you, hopefully, will be able to dig yourself out of your hole before you get in too deep to do so. Nobody wants to be stuck in a hole.

Now it's your turn. How do you want to proceed?

Speaking of going to the doctor. Let's get some testing done. **Turn the page** for **Testing—My Personal Story.**

Still wondering if you're grieving the right way? Or headed down a slippery slope? Turn to **page 55** for **There Is No Right Way to Grieve.**

Still feeling bad? Maybe you need to **Do More Good Sh!t** to feel better. Turn to **page 147.**

TESTING - MY
PERSONAL STORY

So there I am, sans baby, sans sanity, sans purpose, and sans worth {per society}. And I milked that sh!t like a cow.

Are you upset traffic was terrible trying to get to our meeting? Well, my baby died.

Disappointed they ran out of your favorite frittata? Well, my baby died.

Wish the guy in front of you would get off his phone and just pay for his f'ing groceries? Well, my baby died.

Wanna whine about your kids being brats and not going to bed on time? You guessed it. My baby is dead.

And while my perspective of life {and life's complexities} completely changed for the better {over time, not immediately}, I was a miserable person to be around. I could "Debbie Downer one-up" you all day long—and I would win. Every. Single. D@mned. Time.

And then one day...one day I woke up and realized I was living my life waiting to die. And it sucked. I was constantly asking myself "What is the bare minimum I can do today so I can still say I 'functioned' and then climb into bed as early as humanly possible?"

The life I was living couldn't even be classified as a life. Again, that was fine for me, but I was bringing others down with me. No matter how much of a recluse I became, my husband still had to come home every night to this hot mess. And that wasn't really fair. He had his own grieving to do, his own life to live, his own demons to battle. He didn't need to fight mine for me too.

And, let's be honest, if Madelyn had seen me back in 2015 {even though she would have only been five years old}, she would have {or at least should have} slapped me so hard my head would still be spinning today.

Literally, one morning I woke up and something in my brain had flipped. I had my light bulb, aha moment. I was NOT going to continue to live my life waiting to die to be with my baby again. I was too chicken to take my own life, so I might as well make the life I had worth living.

Now, HOW do I make it worth living? I. Don't. Know. But living in bed, hiding from anything and everything that could hurt me {or bring me pleasure for that matter}, and turning into Jabba the Hutt couldn't be the answer...

So I started taking baby "testing" steps.

I would make it a goal to shower once a week—then twice a week—then I was almost showering every day {now, washing my hair and/or putting on clothes or makeup were totally different stories—again, baby steps}.

So, I just spent aaaaaaaaaaaaaaaallllllllllllllllllllllllllll that time and energy showering; what if I went and sat outside in the sun?...If I'm already outside the house, what if I just got in my car?...I'm already in my car, what if I just drove somewhere?...I'm already in the parking lot of the Target; what if I just go in...? {Okay, actually going into Target was a little aggressive and ambitious. Let's try turning around and going to QT for a fountain soda...}

Don't go getting any crazy ideas. Other human people still scared the cr@p outta me. Often just seeing them with a child {of any age} would turn me into a violent crying spectacle in public. And this whole "showering and leaving the house" thing didn't happen over the course of a day—or even a week. It literally took about a year to go from "I think I wanna take a shower" to "Let's just go into Target"...you don't know how many times I would drive to the parking lot, park the car, then turn around and drive right back home.

Now, don't get me wrong—there were still plenty of days that I relapsed into a pile of goo—where taking a shower or even getting out of bed was too much to ask of me. I would be going along just fine, living my day to day...taking baby steps and making little bits of progress only to have the wind knocked out of me by an imaginary elephant sitting on my sternum. When that happened, the only thing I could do was take a second to catch my breath, regroup and reevaluate, and start back over at the beginning with those baby steps—taking everything sixty seconds at a time. That's really all anyone can do.

But {again this is a big BUT} I was moving, ever so slowly, outside of my grief bubble. I was stretching it—in hopes that I would become a living, breathing human again...

Now it's your turn. Where do you want to go?

Do you want the absolute best advice one mortal could ever give another mortal? {I'm totally not blowing this out of proportion.} **Turn the page** to **Write It Down and Work It Out, B!tch.** {No really, I promise, I'm not overselling this.}

Wanna finally finish out this personal story {with the big exciting climax, followed by falling actions and nice resolution—yeah, I've seen a movie too}? And see how I came to terms with my lot in life? Turn to **page 211** for **Acceptance—My Personal Story.**

Think I'm so full of it my eyes should be brown? Let's make a U-turn and go back to **page 93** to remind you that **I Am Your Grief Guru.**

WRITE IT DOWN AND WORK IT OUT, B!TCH

You're probably wondering why this title packs such a punch. Three reasons:

1. I wanted to get your attention. Do I have it now? This is important.
2. You can't end a sentence in a preposition. That's like the only grammar rule I know. But, I don't actually know what a preposition is…so, if in doubt, I just add b!tch to the end. Fixes the nonexistent problem every time.
3. You didn't think a thirty-something (er, I mean, twenty-three…yeah, I'm twenty-three years old,) could go an entire book without making a Brit-Brit reference, did you?

————————————— Word to the Wise —————————————

If you only read one chapter of this whole book, it should be this one. These two activities (in connection with being READY for them: see This Might Not Be Your Time on page 83) completely changed the trajectory of my post-Madelyn life. It's no secret I was a hot mess after Maddie's death {and not the HOT kind of hot mess either}.

As I've already said, it took me several years to get to where I could see past the end of my nose {I blame a lot of that on medication, hormones, stress, and life events…} to get to where I could look toward tomorrow—not just surviving the next few seconds.

After Madelyn's death I gained sixty pounds {I didn't move and ate my emotions.}. While I've never been supermodel skinny, if you put sixty unnecessary pounds on anyone, they'll feel it. For a very long time, I couldn't care less. My outsides were reflecting how I felt on my insides. I was a worthless blob of flesh and bones; the world might as well know it at a glance.

No one in my life was willing to tell me "no" or that maybe (just maybe) I should consider going on a walk instead of inhaling that spiral sliced ham. Honestly, I don't blame them—I probably would have tried to cut their car's break lines if they even thought about making a comment like that.

One day, at the beginning of a new year, a friend shared about a contest through a local radio station. The "winners," based on their brief essay, would get six weeks of free personal training at a local gym. Then, the person who lost the largest percentage of body fat would get the rest of the year at the gym comped.

So, I wrote up my sob story about how worthless of a human being I was and how being skinny and pretty would cure all my problems {remember My Grief Can Beat Up Your Grief} and hit submit.

Obviously, I got a call about a week later saying I won the essay contest and it's time to get started in the gym.

———————————— Side Note ————————————
I later saw the submissions of the other "winners." My sob story definitely beat the others out of the water...

So, I started going to the gym to meet with my personal trainer three mornings a week {Okay, "morning" is a very loose term. Technically, 11:30 a.m. is still morning}. My competitive spirit—::anything you can do, I can do better::—wanted to show I could actually pull this off.

While I ended up coming in second in the weight loss contest {I lost eighteen pounds in six weeks—then immediately gained it back because, well, donuts}, I also learned leaving the house and going to the gym wasn't completely and utterly sucktastic.

Up to this point I wasn't really leaving the house at all. Anxiety was my best worst enemy. Being around other people scared me and having to actually TALK to other people made my head spin just thinking about it.

Here's why I recommend going to the gym to anyone who needs a little {and I mean a very little} kick in the pants:

- Going to the gym got me out of the house—something I needed a real reason to do those days—{working out in the living room just doesn't offer the same "out of the house" feature}.

- I had to put on clothes to go to the gym...but not *real* clothes. A sports bra and spandex pants, but at least they were CLEAN pants and a bra. A huge step up from a three-day-old sweatshirt stained with chocolate and tears.
- Even though I DID have to put on clothes, I DIDN'T have to "get ready." Hair in a high pony and no makeup. Perfectly, lazily, easy. "Getting ready" could no longer be an excuse to not go.
- While there *were* other people at the gym, I didn't have to actually *talk* to any of them. Everyone kinda keeps to themselves at the gym (most of the time with headphones). For a long time I wore a broken pair of headphones just so people thought I was "in the zone" and wouldn't try to talk to me. I didn't want the stimulation of music—but I also didn't want anyone to feel like they could talk to me, win-win.
- Having those other people there—while still slightly stress-inducing—also added some accountability. There were a few people who had the same gym routine as I had. You start to recognize faces and do the "I acknowledge your existence" head bob when you see them {don't worry, no words were actually exchanged}.
- If I didn't show up, even though no names or personal details are ever shared, those familiar faces would give me the disapproving "where were you" head tilt the next time we saw each other. It always made me feel a little bad—like I let them down.
- Paying someone to hold you accountable and make you move {a personal trainer} is a huge motivator to NOT blow off your appointment because you want to sleep. {This theory is similar to my "everyone needs a therapist" theory.}

- I don't care who is, or is not, in the gym with you. It is generally frowned upon to curl up on the treadmill and take a nap...so you might as well move. Even if you're moving one mph on the elliptical or lifting two-pound weights on the bench press, you are still moving your body—I can all but guarantee that is far more than you'd be doing if you were at home lying in bed.

It's been YEARS since I started going to the gym, and I still see a personal trainer a couple times a week. While my weight hasn't really changed {I still love Oreo cookies}, I know I'm a healthier person, have more muscle mass, better stamina, and have kept from being a five-hundred-pound blobby ball of fat.

Also, that baby step of going to the gym regularly has translated into my being open to trying other experiences, meeting new people, and doing new things. Things I just know I never would have done {or even considered} had it not been for me doing as little as humanly possible but also leaving the house...

*****

The second thing I started doing was journaling. But not the "dear diary" kind of seventh grade girl journaling. A blank sheet of paper was, and still is, completely overwhelming to me. I did something I like to call bullet POINT journaling {not to be confused with just bullet journaling—that also takes waaaaaay too much work and creativity}.

Each night before I got into bed I wrote down the three things I was grateful for that day, and the three things I did right...

It's not as easy as it sounds {but it is so much more meaning-ful…}. I worked hard to focus on JUST the past twenty-four hours and to NOT repeat my "gratefuls" or "did rights" from day to day.

This small act each night helped to keep me focused on the present moment (not in the past or future), which helped me calm my self-induced unnecessary suffering and allowed me to realize that I wasn't a completely useless waste of space.

Yes, my "gratefuls" were entirely materialistic. If you read my journal without any context, you would have thought I was a princess with her nose in the air…but it kept me in the moment, in the present, and out of my own {hateful, vicious} mind. My "gratefuls" included things like the extra {free} shot of espresso in my coffee, the complete stranger who held the door open for me when my arms were full, the front row parking space, and getting extra time before bed to finish that really good book. None of the things I wrote down were earth-shattering—but journaling helped to remind me it doesn't have to be something epic to be grateful for it. You can be grateful for the mundane yet out of the ordinary.

This nightly journaling practice started to snowball—which lead to an avalanche. I started carrying my journal around with me so I could write down my "did rights" and "gratefuls" on the spot, so I wouldn't have to try to remember them all day. My three bullet points turned into five, or however many I had that day. I started writing down random thoughts throughout the day too, tracking my water intake, creating a "want to do" list, and even started long form journaling {…Dear Diary, today the boy in fifth period looked over at me while I was looking at him. OMG I was so embarrassed *::all the "i's" dotted with hearts and stars::*}.

I found I was perversely excited to see how quickly I could fill in my "three things" each day—so I could continue adding more. I started making lists of things that made me smile for when I was having a rough day {the TV show *Get Smart*, early 2000s frat boy rap, a "long soda" and listening to the rain}. Things I wanted to do in my life {see the ball drop in NYC on NYE, touch a puffin, go to auctioneer school—and flair bartending school, spend twenty-four-plus hours in Vegas without a hotel room…}.

This journal became a living, breathing thing to me. It was just as {if not more} important than my cell phone, and I felt naked without it. That very first, handmade "grateful-did right" journal is what inspired me to create The Sharing Solace Gratitude Journal—to help others stay in the present and choose to see the happy in their life too.

While I know these "baby steps" probably won't work for everyone {to be completely honest, I sure didn't think they would work for me either}, I *really* believe you should give them a try—if even just for just a little while—only if it's so you can tell me you proved me wrong…

Now it's your turn. You decide where to go next:

Looking for more tips to stay present and in the moment? Turn right back around to **page 147** for **Do More Good Sh!t.**

Turn the page if you want to play a game. I like to call it **Two Truths {and a Lie}.**

Need a little more motivation to find your new normal and new happy? **Hey Baby, Let's Go to Vegas!** on **page 231.**

If you were told to skip over here from **Acceptance— My Personal Story**, time to go back to **page 211.**

TWO TRUTHS {AND A LIE}

Here's something it took me a long, loooooooooooooooong time to realize. Two truths can exist in the same space and in the same moment. And here's the thing: those two truths can completely contradict each other. It's THAT dichotomy that eluded me for so long.

I thought:

- Because I was sad and grieving the death of my daughter, I was not allowed to be happy...like ever.
- Because I was pissed off that science couldn't "fix" my genetics to the point that I could have happy, healthy babies, I couldn't also marvel in the amazing medical accomplishments already available {like even having the ability to know what was wrong with me and for the process of in vitro fertilization}.
- Because I hated the universe and what it had "done" to me, I couldn't also love the beautiful nature it had created— that helped me feel grounded and brought me back to life.
- Because I wasn't able to have my own healthy children, I couldn't auntie the hell out of, and enjoy, my nephews for who they are.

It's easy to get caught up in your feelings of sadness and sorrow, especially in those early days of grief...but don't let that overarching sentiment over*reach* its boundaries. You can be sad, and also allow yourself to smile when your favorite song comes on the radio, do the crossword because it brings you joy, or take a hot bath because it soothes your soul.

It took me way too long to realize that finding joy in my life after Madelyn's death did not dishonor her. It was probably MORE dishonoring to live out the rest of my life miserable. I finally allowed myself to travel, read "mind candy" novels, sit by the pool, watch bad '80s movies, and even make meaningful memories with her cousins. All of those brought me pleasure—and just because I was finding pleasure in my everyday life, it didn't mean I loved my daughter any less.

Think about someone you care for very deeply, maybe a spouse, a best friend, a child, a parent... If you were to spontaneously combust tomorrow and be gone forever, would you want that person to be sad every second of every day for the rest of their life? No! {At least, I hope not.} You would want them to mourn your death...for the appropriate amount of time...then move forward toward their new happy. If that's what *you* want for them, don't you believe that the one you lost feels the same way?

I cannot, in good faith, think my Madelyn would want me to shun my nephews because she is not here to play with them too. I can be sad she is not here to make them play "Multinational Conglomerate CEO" with her {she would NOT be playing house} and also be happy, and honored, to see those boys grow up to become men.

─────────── And Now for the Lie ───────────

I promised you a lie {the two truths being anything you want them to be, co-existing together on the same space-time continuum}. The lie is: this grief thing gets easier. It doesn't get easier {though some think it starts to *feel* a little easier—that's why people say it}. You get stronger, you're able to carry it better and with less strain. And, the grief you're carrying just gets different. Read Grocery Bag Grief on page 245 if you don't get what I'm saying. The grief doesn't get easier. You get stronger.

───

Now it's your turn. You pick where you wanna go:

Still think I'm crazy? {You've read an awful lot of a crazy person's musings if that's the case.} **Turn the page** and **Go Duck Yourself.**

This is a tough concept to grasp {especially if you're not in the right head space for it, your brain could have just exploded...} Let's turn to **page 69** and **Just F'ing Breathe.**

Maybe we should go back and take a look at **Grief Shaming and Victim Blaming** on **page 125.** Are you Grief Shaming yourself and not allowing yourself the possibility of joy?

GO DUCK YOURSELF

———

They say you have to have truly mastered a subject to be able to teach it {and as someone who has half-@$$ed more than one presentation in her life, I absolutely agree with that statement}. No, I'm not going to ask you to go teach others how to grieve…for some reason that makes me think of teaching a toddler who is just mastering vocabulary curse words—fun for a while, but then you've basically ruined the toddler's life…

Here's a concept I first heard about from my hubby, who's a techie. It was presented in *The Pragmatic Programmer*[7] by Andrew Hunt and David Thomas. While the book itself sounds as mind-numbingly boring as watching linoleum curl—this story really appealed to me {maybe that's because I now had a reason to tell my husband to "go duck yourself" and actually mean it}.

So here's the concept as I know it {remember, I haven't actually read the book—I can pass out from boredom on my own without reading your book—thankyouverymuch}:

———

7   Hunt, Andrew and David Thomas. *The Pragmatic Programmer: From Journeyman to Master*. Addison Wesley Longman, Inc., 2000.

A computer programmer was "developing away" one day and having a very tough time debugging some of the code. He {let's assume he's a dude} spends hours going through the code line by line, letter by letter...he's absolutely stumped. Finally, he pushed away from his desk and went over to his coworker and started word vomiting about his problem, the background, how he implemented it, and the bug—then stops mid-sentence. "Never mind, I got it." He walks away and fixes the problem without using {or even getting} anyone's input.

The next day, one day closer to his deadline, he is busy tip-py-typing away on his program—coding like a fiend—when he runs into ANOTHER issue. No matter what he does, he cannot find a solution. So, again, he marches back over to his coworker and starts laying it all out, again. After {what feels like} hours of super-villain-style monologue-ing, BOOM a flash of insight happens. He stops, turns around, marches back to his desk {now a little embarrassed he didn't see his solution earlier}, and corrects the issue.

Day three, D-Day, the Moby Dick of bugs shows up and he *has* to get this thing done... So, over to his co-worker he goes in a huff, totally ticked that he has *another* issue he can't solve.

Before he can even get a word out of his mouth, his colleague looks at him and says "Dude, I'm super, super, super busy right now. I have my own work to do that's gotta get done today. I don't have time. But I got you something." And she tosses him a yellow rubber ducky.

"Okay...? I don't think you understand. I don't have time for a bubble bath! I have important stuff I'm doing, and I need your help," he says.

She says, "No, you really don't. I haven't helped you yet—I haven't even gotten a word in edgewise. Just explain what you're doing and the problems you're having to the duck."

So he goes back to his desk and, like a complete idiot, starts explaining everything, every little nuance, to this little rubber ducky. And, surprise, surprise! In explaining the program, the issue, and all the other little bits and pieces out loud he finds the problem, fixes it, and saves the day!

This story isn't just some techie-nerd urban legend. This is a legitimate business practice and a "life" thing. If you can find a way to deconstruct the issues you're struggling with, you may just find you have the answers you didn't know you had. If you have a problem {any type of problem} that you understand intimately, try explaining it to someone {or something—like a ducky} that has absolutely no experience with it. More often than not, you will "accidentally" figure out a solution to your issue by dumbing it down and thinking it through.

Rarely are our issues so complex that we don't understand what is going on or don't have the knowledge to problem solve it. We're probably just too well versed in what we're dealing with that we try to nit-pick it to death and "can't see the forest for the trees."

Sometimes just speaking your thoughts, feelings, and emotions out loud helps you to process them. Sometimes you actually have to hear yourself say the syllables out loud before it really resonates that **that's** what you're thinking and feeling.

I don't expect your rubber ducking to solve all your problems {remember, grief is not a problem you solve}. But I believe it will help you clarify, for yourself, what you're feeling. It may remind you that you're stronger than you think and have been through more then you realize...

So get yourself a yellow rubber ducky and get after it. Go Duck Yourself!

Now it's your turn. You decide how you'd like to move forward:

Think I'm crazy? {I'm not, my mother had me tested.} Try it anyway—then **turn the page** to remember **This Is Not a Test.**

Or, maybe you don't know where you fall on the **Kvetching Sphere** and just need to b!tch a little—turn to **page 109** for a reminder.

Like the techie-ness of this story? Want more mumbo-jumbo and equations? Turn to **page 243** to learn all about **Happiness.**

THIS IS NOT A TEST

I think many childhoods looked like mine. Pretty much everything you did prepared you for the next thing: you practiced for the big game, you rehearsed so you remembered your lines opening night, you studied so you "knocked it outta the park" on the final exam. Everything you did in life set you up for the next "bigger, better thing."

Even as an adult—I'm constantly working on my "one step ahead"...once I {hurry up and} finish this one thing, it can springboard me into the next thing/project/promotion/job/activity/role...

In junior high school, with all my scrunchies, neon-colored gel pens, and JanSport backpack, I was at the pinnacle of my cool. Between choir, theater, and my group of friends that called ourselves the "mixed fruits," I was just too much to handle. {We even all had different "fruit names"—I was "something that is rutabaga red."}

As a complete theater nerd, I spent every day after school in the gym-itorium "perfecting my craft." One year we did a cute little one-act play titled *This Is a Test* by Stephen Gregg. {The perfect length and emotional level for thirteen- to fifteen-year-old kids.} Even all these years later it sticks in my mind…for no reason other than its "catchy chorus."

There was a "choir" of three at the back of the stage dressed in all black that every few minutes would hold up an object {pen, book, test, chicken, shoe, etc.} and recite:

Thing 1: This is a pen.
Thing 2 and 3: A what?
Thing 1: A pen.
Thing 2 and 3: A what?
Thing 1: A pen.
Thing 2 and 3: Oh, a pen.

Needless to say, for the rest of the school year {and beyond—even to this day, decades later}, my friends and I would hold up random things and sing the chorus! {…because we were thirteen (and still act like) idiots who had all the time in the world…}

So now, anytime I think of tests {real, imaginary, or of the emergency broadcast system}, I can't help but think of my thirteen-year-old self and that silly little play.

One thing I constantly recited to myself after Madelyn's death:

Thing 1: This is not a test.
Thing 2 and 3: A what?
Thing 1: Not a test.
Thing 2 and 3: A what?
Thing 1: Not a test.
Thing 2 and 3: Oh, not a test.

This. Is. Not. A. Test. This is not a lesson; this is not school. You haven't studied for this. You cannot pass or fail. No one is setting you up. This. Is. Not. A. Test.

If you see your loss and grief as a test, then one can only assume you believe you could have been more prepared for it—even if it was a "pop quiz." You could have studied harder, reviewed your notes, paid better attention in "class"…or even cheated off your neighbor's paper.

Your loss is not a test. You couldn't have "prepared" any more than you had, you couldn't have gotten a better grade, and you couldn't have cheated your way out of it. Loss is Life {and Life is Loss}. Your loss is just that—a loss. Please understand that {and don't try to make it any more or less than that}. Experience it, feel it, and move forward (coming back to those feels anytime you need).

Don't try to guilt yourself out of grief.

I think Tim Lawrence, author of the article "Everything Doesn't Happen for A Reason," said it best:

> *Your loss is not a test.*
> *Your loss is not a lesson.*
> *Your loss is not a gift.*
> *Your loss is a loss.*

Now it's your turn. Where do you want to go?

Not quite sure how you feel about your loss? Maybe you need more info. **Turn the page** for **When in Doubt, Get More Information.**

Once you can accept that your loss is just that— a loss, **You'll Set Yourself Free.** And it's an amazing feeling. Turn to **page 223** to see what I mean.

It's okay that you're sad and grieving...over any type of loss. Maybe you need the reminder that **Any Loss Is Grieveable** on **page 45.**

WHEN IN DOUBT, GET MORE INFORMATION

A wise lady once told me: "When in doubt about which path to take, get more information."

Okay, that "wise lady" was my longtime therapist.

{Yes, I see a therapist. Yes, I *regularly* see a therapist. I will shout that from the mountaintops as loud as I can. I think everyone can benefit from speaking to a therapist *and* mentor on a regular basis.}

A few years ago, my therapist and I were discussing my future life as a childless mother. I was second-guessing every decision I'd ever made in my entire life. I was questioning if I was going to regret not raising my own biological children {you know, when I was eighty, and I had no one required to visit me in the nursing home…because I brought them life}.

Kyle and I had exhausted all of our IVF options, but there were still other ways to grow our family {egg donation, surrogacy, fostering, adoption…}, and I was having some very visceral feelings about these "non-biological" options.

Intellectually, I understood that each and every one of these options was viable. Each had their merits and challenges. Each had costs and payoffs... So, what was my deal?!?!

Sometimes {okay, make that most of the time}, the unknown ends up being scarier than what actually happens.

If you're scared, just be scarier than whatever is scaring you!
                                        —THUMPER (FROM *BAMBI*)

Knowledge is power...and power makes you scary...then the transitive property tells us knowledge makes you scarier than whatever scares you.

I spent quite a bit of time exploring all the options. I chatted with friends who were going through the fostering and adoption process. I looked into what it would take, time and money wise, for each of the options. {There was even a time in a coffeeshop where an "adoption broker" was having a meeting with potential clients and I totally eavesdropped and hijacked the conversation to get my questions answered...}

I spent time exploring my emotions. WHY did I have such an immediate reaction when these subjects were brought up? Why did I {almost} always tear up and shut down? Exploring those emotions was also a very important part of the "information gathering" process.

While I can't say with 100 percent certainty that I've made the right decision, I CAN say that I explored all of my options, took each bit of information {facts, figures, *and* emotions} into account, and made the best decision for me and my little family of three.

There is ALWAYS more information you can gather before making a decision {especially a big one}. There is always someone else you can talk to, a book you can read, a website you can explore, an expert you can refer to. If you don't feel ready to make a decision then gather more information! {But remember, don't let the information gathering *keep* you from making a decision! That's "analysis paralysis."}

———————————— Side Note ————————————

I'm not pretending this was a decision I made solely on my own. This was very much a joint decision between me and my husband. Also, I don't want to put words in his mouth, so I'm only speaking of my decision process.

Whatever decision you choose to make, I want you to remember something {yes, I'm saying it again, because it bears repeating}:

You made the best possible decision you could with the facts and information you had available to you at the time. You cannot beat yourself up because new information came to light after the fact {new information will *always* find a way to come to light}.

Now it's your turn. You decide where to go next:

Let's move forward. **Turn the page** to read about my acceptance in **Acceptance—My Personal Story.**

Remember, you've already given yourself the **Permission** to feel your feels, explore your options, and provide yourself the self-care you need. If you need to hear it again, turn to **page 51.**

Maybe you need to **Just F'ing Breathe**—this sh!t is tough to hear and even tougher to internalize. Turn to **page 69.**

ACCEPTANCE - MY PERSONAL STORY

Acceptance is a fickle b!tch. It's one of those things you just kinda slowly ease into—so slowly that you don't really realize what happened until you're well on your way to your "new normal."

Here's my take on a quote someone shared with me—that was shared with them by someone else—that was shared with them a third time (and probably so on and so on and so on)—that was found on a message board somewhere. While I can't attribute this idea to anyone specific {and I'm sure I've butchered the original idea while turning it into my own}, it really shows just how grief, and acceptance, work:

Grief comes in waves. When your loss first happens, it's like you went down with the Titanic. You're drowning. There are bits and pieces of wreckage all around you. You grasp for anything that will help you keep your head above water—and everything, as far as the eye can see, reminds you of the beauty and majesty of what once was. The waves, a hundred feet tall, refuse to cease. Over. And over. And over. And over. Mercilessly. The waves ignore your screams to let you catch your breath and get your bearings. All you can do is hold on, and pray you make it to tomorrow.

Over time the storm, ever so slowly, begins to retreat. The waves are still a hundred feet high, but they give a little reprieve between each swell. They allow you to catch your breath— allow you to function. You start to be able to time the waves, anticipate their arrival—not every single time but occasionally.

As you continue to move farther from the storm; farther from the wreckage—and more time passes after your loss—the height of the waves begins to decrease. First ninety feet, then seventy...farther and farther apart the waves become. You will forever be in this ever-moving ocean but you're learning to live with it.

That's not to say a tidal wave won't surprise you from time to time—but you will have an idea of how to handle it when it does come. You don't panic like you once did. You know you will come through that wave, to the other side, in one piece and be able to come up for a breath of fresh air.

There are many things that got me on the path—to start contemplating—beginning to move toward—thinking about— wanting to—accept the hand I was dealt. {Yeah, I know that's kinda hard to follow...but it's fitting. I think that is how many of us move into the "acceptance" phase...little by little, tiny thought by tiny thought, almost fighting to stay back in the depression.}

If you haven't yet, it could be worth reading Write It Down and Work it Out, B!tch on page 185 as this was really my "turning point." I found a way to be out among the living without actually having to interact with anyone. And journaling kept my mind in the present moment {mostly} and out of the "should haves" and "what ifs."

I think what *really* got me to consider accepting that my Madelyn was dead was this quote:

> *When a child is born, it is the mother's instinct to protect the baby. When a child dies, it is the mother's instinct to protect their memory.*
>
> —UNKNOWN

There is just something about seeing a quote {even when that quote is unattributed}. For some reason, it makes your feelings feel more real and validated—like it's acceptable for you to have them. It helps you realize that you're not the only one that's experienced what you're going through. Someone else has experienced this *and* thought enough about that experience to put words to it. I've always taken solace in finding and reading relatable quotes—which is probably why I share so many of them on my social media pages.

──────────── Warning ────────────

I'm gonna jump around a little bit here but stay with me, it'll come back around and make perfect sense in the end…I hope…

I'd lived the last several years of my life {pretty much since 2010} behind a veil. I'd grown way too accustomed to making split second character decisions. When you're a woman of a certain age, like me, complete strangers have no problem prying into your personal life.

The line of questioning almost always goes like this:

- What's your name?
- What do you do?
- How many kids do you have?

I just *know* that question is coming when I meet someone new—and given that my job before Sharing Solace was all about "kissing babies and shaking hands," I met a LOT of new people... When the question was asked I had two options:

1. Straight up lie to them and tell them I had no kids {while ripping away a little piece of my soul at the same time for not speaking my truth—and Madelyn's name} or,
2. Tell them that my only child is dead—which normally led to a barrage of questions and/or a cry-fest {again, with a complete stranger—often in a parking lot, or a lobby of some sort...not where you really want to be having that kinda conversation}.

I got really "good" at judging people on first impressions: Do I intend to keep the relationship superficial and lie to them now to save them the uncomfortable-ness of hearing about my dead baby and my inability to have children {all the while shredding my heart into a billion pieces each time I choose not to speak about Madelyn}? Or, do I get *really* painfully awkward *really* fast by introducing myself as the lady whose babies die?

Basically, do I instantly write them off as not "worthy" of a relationship and lie to them now, making the situation more socially acceptable? Or, do I get really weird really quickly by telling them the truth—potentially scaring them off?

Acceptance, to me, came in the form of being able to speak my truth {without always starting a pity party}. Because of learning to speak that new truth, a business grew—but more than *just* a business. A passion and a mission to help other grievers feel less lonely and isolated as they traversed their own unique grief path. My acceptance story just happens to have a name. It's called "Sharing Solace."

Sharing Solace allows me to feel comfortable living my "new normal" authentically. It allows me to stand up in a room full of complete strangers and say: "Hi, I'm Crystal Webster and I'm the (co)Founder and CSO (Chief Solace Officer) of Sharing Solace—helping grievers grieve and lovers love their griever. We help those traversing grief realize they are NOT alone, they are NOT crazy, and this IS normal. Not every day is a good day, but there is good in every day. Sharing Solace helps you to 'Remember. You're not alone.'"

While I don't specifically speak Madelyn's name immediately, people don't just "hang out with sad people because it's fun." The follow-up question I often get is "What led you down this path?" THEN I get to speak about Maddie—in a way I believe brings hope and comfort to others.

So, my acceptance story IS The Sharing Solace Story. It is a hard story to tell, mostly because it's hard to decipher where "Madelyn and Mommy" ends and "Sharing Solace" begins. That line between personal and professional is so blurred that it's more of a blob—or a lens that colors everything rose going forward.

Obviously, I always knew my Madelyn Elizabeth was special {and the most beautiful baby in the whole wide world…again, I *may* be a little bit biased}. Her energy was palpable from the second she was conceived. Her soul touched more lives in her eight brief hours on Earth than I can ever hope to in my (hopefully) eighty-plus years here…

From the moment I felt that last bit of life drain from Madelyn's body I knew, just knew, I had to do something to honor her life and her legacy. At the time, I thought my idea was novel. Turns out, the quote above proves most mamas need to protect their baby's memory. Mamas need that outlet to speak their baby's name with a smile in their heart instead of *just* a tear in their eye.

Once you are able to find a purpose for your pain—whether that be a business, a nonprofit, a tradition or ritual, or a safe space to speak their name without tears of sadness—it is then that you are able to move toward acceptance.

Now it's your turn. You pick where you wanna go:

Want to know more about Sharing Solace, and why it's so special and symbolic to me and so many others? Turn to **page 251** for **The Sharing Solace Story.**

Just because I've learned to accept Madelyn's death doesn't mean it always feels good. **Turn the page** to see why **Grief Is a Broken Rib.**

Need a reminder that doubt and acceptance can go hand in hand? Turn to **page 205** for **When in Doubt, Get More Information.**

Or, that acceptance and pain can coexist at the same moment in time? Turn to **page 193** for **Two Truths {and a Lie}.**

GRIEF IS A BROKEN RIB

{I'm speaking from experience here...both with grief and broken ribs—both are terrible...}

You don't just break a rib—it's not like you just misstep, or sleep wonky, or tweak something and **oops** you've broken a rib. Something powerful has to HAPPEN {not like that mysterious bruise on my shin that just won't go away}; you get in a fight, fall down a flight of stairs, get kicked by a horse... something *powerful* happens. You *know* what happens.

When you break your ribs, the wind is instantly knocked out of you; you're dazed; you don't quite remember who {or where} you are. You know you need help, but you don't know what to ask for—or have the breath to do it. Your life flashes before you in a split second. You stare like a deer in headlights hoping someone saw what just happened and will come help you—out of the goodness of their heart.

The doctors can give you some medication to help try to ease the pain, but other than that there's not much that can be done. All they can really do is confirm what you already know: you're in an incredible amount of pain. You're just going to have to "power through."

While healing, your chest aches, it's heavy. Getting out of bed is a chore, taking a shower is not gonna happen, not even a little bit. Sitting hurts, laying down throbs, standing up is the worst pain imaginable. You try to take your mind off the pain and "do something—do anything," but you are so easily distracted—if the pain allows you to focus at all. You sit and stare and just try to focus on your breathing {which, by the way, hurts too}.

Over time, you begin to learn to live with the pain—avoiding certain situations, abstaining from physical activity, laughing, coughing—until the mind-numbing pain begins to subside and you find your new normal way of life. There are still things you don't like to do because no matter how you do it, it's still painful. You do everything in your power to not sneeze—but sneezing doesn't fill your soul with impending dread any longer.

At some point, you start to realize that your excruciating pain is more of a dull ache now, and you are not constantly reminded of the "powerfulness" of what initially happened. That *painful* pain only rears its ugly head when it's going to rain, or you roll over in your sleep wrong, or you have the hiccups. There are even ever-so-slight glimpses of you forgetting about your pain altogether—but a "friendly" reminder is never too far away.

Over time you're able to smile again—and even laugh—just in general…AND about the time you "went 'sledding' in the Swiss Alps and broke, like, all your ribs and took the creepy pedophile ambulance van to the ER where the doctor didn't even speak German (the national language) very well, so you went through the cabinets and pointed at the medication and supplies you wanted him to give you—and he did…"

You always remember the pain is there, and sometimes you're reminded at the worst possible time or place…but it's manageable {sometimes only with the help of medication}… and your sad tears begin to become interspersed with happy tears…And your chest begins to only hurt when it rains.

―――――――――――――――――― Side Note ――――――――――――――――――

This story was originally a blog post on SharingSolace.com— so it might sound a little bit familiar. I've expanded and made some changes here. I thought it was too good not to share again…

Now it's your turn. How do you want to proceed?

Don't like this grief metaphor? Fine. I got another one you might like better: check out **Grocery Bag Grief** on **page 245.**

You'll Set Yourself Free remembering where you've been and how strong you've become by overcoming those obstacles. **Turn the page.**

Or, maybe after reading this very enlightening piece you want the reminder that **I Am Your Grief Guru** by turning to **page 93.**

YOU'LL SET YOURSELF FREE

Here is something I absolutely, in my wildest dreams, never expected to happen. It seems so backward and counterintuitive:

A huge weight has been lifted from my life since my Madelyn died. {Stay with me. I promise I'll start to make some sense here in a minute.} When Madelyn died, I was wrecked. I was broken into a million, billion tiny pieces. Duh, that's just a given. My words felt meaningless, my actions thoughtless... I had fewer than zero reasons to get out of bed, until one day I did.

There was a day that I realized I could put things into {my own} perspective. The worst possible thing I could ever imagine happening to a person was the sudden tragic death of a child (followed by the death of the life you saw for them, and for yourself with them).

At one point in my grief I actually made a laundry list of all the terrible, horrible, no good, very bad things I thought could happen to a person {dismemberment, job loss, terminal illness diagnosis, divorce, wrongful incarceration...the list went on and on}. I thought through each and every one of these scenarios extensively: who else was affected, the time frame, the short-term effects, the long-term effects. And I decided {again, this is my perspective} that the worst possible thing that could happen to a person was to {knowingly or unknowingly} kill the person you intrinsically love most in this world, essentially making yourself barren, affecting everyone around you with that pain for the rest of their life, while carrying the grief and guilt of what you did with you for the rest of eternity.

Basically, after a whole lot of "research," I decided the death of my Madelyn was my own worst nightmare playing out in real life. That the death of your child, the child you created in love and subsequently (and unknowingly) killed was the worst possible thing that could ever happen to a human being on the face of the planet.

———————————————— Side Note ————————————————

There is a commercial that plays on loop on late night TV for a pediatric hospital. In it, soliciting for donations, a mother says to the camera: "The worst thing you can ever hear is someone telling you your child has cancer."

While I absolutely believe that to be her truth, every single time I see that commercial I scream at the TV, "Bullsh!t! The worst thing you can ever hear is 'Madelyn Elizabeth Webster {insert your child's name here} time of death 4:23 a.m.'" There is some {maybe not a lot but some} hope with cancer. Dead is final.

———————————————————————————————————————

So I sat in my own "self-pity party stew" for a long time. Comparison-itis-ing my grief to everyone else. Brushing theirs off because "at least" this, that, or the other...until one day.

One day I realized I was still {somewhat} upright—I wasn't dead yet, so it must have made me stronger...{Thank you, platitudes.} And my tune changed a little bit {though I was still playing the blues}. I realized that—even after all the "research" {completely unbiased, I might add} was done—the worst possible thing that could ever happen to a human had happened to me. And I still wasn't dead.

For some reason that gave me a little extra pep in my step. It helped me to see the day a little differently.

That extra-long wait to check out at the grocery store? Not the worst thing to ever happen to me.

The screwed up delivery order? I'm still alive.

The traffic and construction that just won't let up? I survived *that*, I'll survive this.

I could LITERALLY look at ANYTHING that happens in my day and say to myself, "This is not the worst thing to ever happen to me."

There is something ridiculously freeing about walking through your day and knowing that whatever stupid cr@p is thrown at you {your boss's unrealistic expectations, the heel of your shoe snapping off, getting into a fender bender}, you'll survive—AND you've survived 100 percent of your days up to this point.

Now it's your turn. You decide how you'd like to move forward:

Did I make you mad with this story because I think **My Grief Can Beat Up Your Grief**? I understand; turn to **page 143.**

Let's go on a Trip! **Turn the page** to welcome yourself to "Paris" in **Hallo Aus Der Schweiz.**

Or, maybe you need a friendly reminder we all process our grief differently and that **There Is No Right Way to Grieve.** Turn to **page 55.**

HALLO AUS DER SCHWEIZ

——

I read an essay by Emily Perl Kingsley a few years back titled "Welcome to Holland."[8] It's about a lady that equated her life with a child with severe autism to a vacation overseas. While it sounds super trite, it was actually really profound—maybe a little extra profound for me... I continued to think and build on that story for a long time—eventually turning it into my own. I'd like to share my version of "the story" with you here:

Imagine your future as a long sabbatical in Paris. You've always wanted to live among the Parisians, enjoy their way of life, take in the culture, eat the cheese and champagne and crepes—oh lordy, those crepes. You want to immerse yourself in the art and history. You really love all things Paris.

To prepare for your time overseas, you study art and fashion, join message boards with locals, teach yourself French {or at least enough French to get by and not look like a total idiot— you figure you'll really pick up the rest when you get there}, you find a perfect flat to live in and wardrobe to match. Then, you make a list of all the places you want to visit and things

---

8   Kingsley, Emily. "Welcome to Holland." 1987.

you want to experience. You pack your bags and board the long flight across the Atlantic.

Right before touching down, after hours and hours in a cramped plane seat, the pilot comes over the intercom and announces, "Willkommen in der Schweiz."

"That's not French," you say to yourself…but you're exhausted from not sleeping on the flight—plus these international flights…they say everything in about fourteen languages… Finally, you hear it. In English: "Welcome to Switzerland."

You panic! WTF? YOU'RE GOING TO PARIS. That's where you signed up to go. You land and you don't know what to do. You were SUPPOSED to be in Paris—the land of baguettes and berets.

Apparently, there's been a change in plans…and you really only have one option. You stay. You adjust. You get some new guidebooks, pick up some Swiss German {not a "real language," btw}, find a chalet to live in, learn to love Raclette and Rösti, and take up skiing.

This place is nothing like Paris. It's slower-paced, not as glamorous, but also less maintenance and flashy. You explore places you didn't even know existed, devour Swiss chocolate by the kilo, and enjoy some of the most beautiful nature in the world. You start to truly appreciate the attention to detail, precision, and perfectionism of the Swiss.

This is not the sabbatical you had planned. You don't get to go home and tell all your friends about your fantabulous time in Paris. It will always hurt a little that you didn't quite get that experience—that future—you so had your heart set on. {You were *almost* as excited to tell people about your experience in Paris after you returned as you were to actually *have* the experience.}

Everyone you know seems to be coming and going from Paris, talking about their amazing trip—the Eiffel Tower, the Louvre, Montmartre. Each time you hear a conversation about the "City of Love," your heart aches, just a little. You think about the experiences you could have had—should have had, the loss of that dream—the loss of that plan. It's very symbolic to you. You will never fully get over it—so you just have to accept that loss, accept that pain.

But, Switzerland is not a place of despair, depression, and distress. It's a perfectly wonderful place—it offers the highest standard of living in the world. You saw places you didn't even know existed; made friends you didn't even know you wanted. You got an experience not many choose to sign up for…but is just as, if not more, worthwhile.

If you spend your whole life wishing you had gotten married, stayed married, had a family, kept your dream job, not been diagnosed…you'll lose out on your new reality. You'll miss out on the beautiful things you DID get to experience, the friends you made, the lessons you learned, and the stories you DO get to tell now.

Your life, this life, your "fantastic" trip to Switzerland, and the stories you now have in your heart—and to share—are your "new normal."

If you choose to spend the rest of your life mourning the loss of "your Paris plan," you will never be able to truly enjoy your time among the Swiss—who, by the way, are also known for their chocolate and cheese.

Now it's your turn. You decide how to move forward:

Wanna go somewhere else? Let's head west!
Hey Baby, Let's Go to Vegas! Turn the page.

Grief Is Not a Problem—you need to learn
that, and it's best if you learn to love the grief
too. Turn to **page 139** for the reminder.

Or, maybe another friendly reminder of **The Needs
of Mourning**? To remind you it's okay to mourn {and
how best to mourn} your loss. Turn to **page 73.**

HEY BABY, LET'S GO TO VEGAS!

———

I. Love. Las. Vegas!! If I could move there, I would {Okay, I probably wouldn't move there because living somewhere means obligations, which means work, which means not vacation…but I tell everyone I would because I love it that much!}

——————— Before We Get Too Far into This ———————
I'm probably going to ramble a little bit. Please indulge me. I promise this story has a point {and a pretty good one at that}. Besides Madelyn, and my husband, the thing I love most in this world is Sin City—so pardon me if I get a little excited. Think of this story as your "mind candy" in the book {almost like you're already in Vegas!}…and, as your own personal tour of my happy place.

My love for Vegas started because it was my first real "grown-up" vacation after I got my job right out of college. It also happened to be the place where I got engaged and then went back a year later to get married. Yup, I'm the girl who had a full Catholic Mass wedding on the strip in Sin City. {I promise, those were two different trips over a year apart. I didn't elope or do anything crazy. I feel that's important to specify every time I tell my "I heart LV" story because, well, I'm a girl and I'm impulsive...but I also like to plan out my impulses.}

Since our wedding, Kyle and I have made it a tradition to go back every year for our anniversary. We've only missed our annual pilgrimage twice in the fourteen-plus years we've been married: first because I contracted the measles {that's a whole 'nother story and yes, I was vaccinated} and then because I was two weeks postpartum with Madelyn and was put on bed rest because I had a gaping wound in my abdomen.

Most people think Vegas and think extravagant lifestyles, drunken debauchery, moral corruptness, hookers, strip clubs, the mob, and mortgaging the house for another roll of the dice. Well hell yeah!! Okay, not really. Lemme tell you how I roll {pun intended}:

Day 1: You take the 12-noon direct Southwest flight from Kansas City. It's a three-hour flight and a two-hour time change—getting you in right about 1:00 p.m. local time. Then a fifteen dollar cab ride to the MGM {only because the Lyft pick up makes you walk about a mile in the opposite direction and with 100–150 pounds of suitcase it's not worth it} to check into your $60/night room overlooking the pool. "Unpack" {unzip your suitcase and throw everything on the floor}, set your out of office email and voice mail, and grab some cash before heading down to the casino to put five dollars in some TV show-themed slot machine {*The Monkees* is the best...if you can find it...}. It'll probably be an early-ish night because 10:00 p.m. Vegas time is midnight your body time. It's okay, go to bed. You'll need to bank that sleep. You still have six more days of this.

Oh, but first you need to know what to pack in that 100–150 pounds of suitcase(s)

- Three to five liters of flavored vodka poured into tall skinny Fiji water bottles {because they pack well, don't leak, and are extra thick and strong enough to get smashed up in flight. The plastic Smirnoff bottles work too but rarely do they come in flavors.}. Stay away from glass bottles; they're too heavy and too likely to break.
- Small water bottles that will fit in your purse or pocket. Use these to transfer vodka into once you get there. {If you're super lucky, the hotel with give you a four-ounce bottle of water when you check in, but don't count on it.} Once the flavored vodka has been transferred to these smaller bottles, it is now called "pants vodka"—no matter what that bottle ultimately goes into.

———————————— Pro Tip ————————————

Metal flasks are nice and all, but they get heavy, don't really hold that much, are hard to clean, can't be single use if necessary, and don't glide through metal detectors as nicely as plastic.

- Flip-flops and a swimsuit you wouldn't dare wear in public in the "real world"
- Big floppy pool hat and sunglasses
- Inflatable pool floaties, the more obnoxious the better— but make sure they're flat-ish; otherwise, you'll have to deflate your sparkly unicorn's head to be allowed in the pool

- Protein bars for breakfast and late night "room spinning" snacks
- Twelve one-pound bags of M&Ms
- Light pool reading {aka "pool smut" or "mind candy"... nothing remotely educational or thought provoking}
- Powdered Pedialyte {get a red/pink flavor, the rest are cr@p}
- Cold hard cash {once you run out, you're done gambling— so bring plenty}
- Every makeup and hair product you own—though you won't use anything different than what you normally use at home. You feel like you'll get "all dolled up" at least one night...
- Stripper glitter {lotion and aerosol styles work best}
- Some other stuff, like clothes and underwear, sunscreen, and aloe

Back to Vegas. Day 2: Get up, it'll probably be earlier than you'd like because your body's still on Central Standard Time. Don't worry, this will change very soon. Eat a protein bar, pack your pool bag, put on your wildly inappropriate swimsuit and sunscreen, take a shot {probably a little "hair of the dog" if you did last night right...you've already forgotten to pace yourself for the week} and head down to the pool.

Right now, you *think* you want to burn your skin off but, I promise, by this afternoon you'll want at least a little shade. Strategically position your choice of chairs to take that into account. If you're a big dumb dummy like me, once you get settled in, you'll start blowing up your pool floatie by mouth... only to realize halfway through, the resort has a pump that'll do it for you...if you're willing to stand in line {which is short now because, remember, you're up early Vegas time}. So you get up and get it blown up. You read your *Fifty Shades of Grey/Dan Brown/Shopoholic* book until you're so hot sweat is pouring off you. It's five o'clock somewhere. Time for a drink!

You can either order a twenty-five dollar "leaded" beverage or get a six dollar virgin drink and "lead" it yourself using the "pants vodka" you remembered to pack in your pool bag. Now, and only now that you're freaking hot and "hydrated," is it time to get into the lazy river. Grab your glittered {and not too tall so the lifeguards don't blow their whistle at you} inflatable unicorn, your adult beverage, your floppy "I'm a movie star but you can't recognize who I am" hat, and your shades and run {I do mean run—the cement is on FIRE} to the entrance of the lazy river.

Once you're there, dunk in up to your neck, so that everything gets slippery enough to pull the tube over your head without ripping off your skin {or your bandeau swimsuit top, who needs tan lines!?!}. If you've sized your inflatable properly, there is just enough room between your boobs and your tube to squeeze your drink in, so your hands are free to give high-fives {because you tell everyone in the pool it's your birthday—everyday—and they need to high-five you}. This also helps to keep your drink from getting too hot too quickly {even I don't like warm vodka}.

Now we float, until we can't float no more. Three to five laps at least, unless you've made friends with the strangers floating next to you—then tack on a few extra laps for good measure. Now, it's probably about lunch time and you're getting hungry. Find your pool chair and order lunch from the cabana boy {it's worth the extra $$ in tip to not have to stand in that line on the lava-like concrete!}—and no salad either! Order the burger and fries. Read some more of your "pool smut" book until lunch arrives and gobble it down {in your wildly inappropriate swimsuit and no cover up because that's how we roll in Vegas—no inhibitions!!}.

──────────── Pro Tip ────────────

Get a players club card and charge lunch {and everything else you possibly can} to the room; you'll want the points to rack up for your next trip. {Personally, if I lose a hundred dollars the entire vacation I feel terrible about it, but because I put everything I can on my M-Life card I continue to get good deals on rooms and cash back to spend on meals and such.}

──────────── Pro tip #2 ────────────

Split lunch with whomever you came with. That way you can fill up {further} on fruity adult beverages…plus there's no place to put leftovers anyway.

Now that we're at least two drinks and a burger and fries into the day, it's time for nap #1. Get good and comfy in your chair {it's probably in the shade about now} and doze off while listening to "club hits of the '80s, '90s, and today" playing over the pool sound system. Maybe it's twenty minutes or two hours later…when you wake up, it's time to play Candy Crush on your phone until you're hot enough for round two in the pool.

Round 2 works similarly to round one. Grab another drink from a cabana boy—or drink ice water—no one really knows, or cares, as long as you act like you're having a great time. Hop in the lazy river and away you go! {Don't forget to tell everyone, again, it's your birthday. If they ask, you're twenty-one. If you're up for a challenge—see how many high-fives you can get in a single lap. If you can beat my record of ninety-seven, I'll give you a dollar}.

At this point, you're probably preparing for nap #2…but you need to dry off first because nap #2 is inside. Read some more "smut" while the water almost immediately evaporates off you {Vegas=desert}, then pack up and head up to the room. Housekeeping has done a wonderful job making up your room while you were away, and it's as cold as an icebox compared to the 100*+ temperature outside. You're covered in sunscreen, sweat, and pool water but don't have quite enough energy from your "busy day" to shower just yet… So you flip on cable TV {you don't have it at home, so it's super exciting} and strip down to the *bare* minimum. Even though you were almost instantly dry, your suit is still wet in all the wrong places. Sleep on top of the comforter {because you don't want to sleep in sunscreen, sweat, and pool water later tonight…}

Once you wake up from your fourth-ish hour of sleep for the day, take a shower and get ready for dinner. Remember all those makeup and hair products you brought? Use none of them—just the necessities, if even that—but you must remember the aerosol stripper glitter; it's part of the "Vegas Tourist" uniform.

———————————— Pro Tip ————————————

Bring special "after-sun" lotion. Traditional lotion contains glycerol, which traps the heat in your skin and turns you into the most painful lobster on the face of the planet. It can also lead to second or third degree burns and a trip to the ER… not that it's actually happened to me…

──────────────── Pro Tip #2 ────────────────

When sleeping, either at night or during nap time, dampen a washcloth or hand towel with cool water and lay it on your skin where you got the most sun. It will help to pull out the heat and keep it moist {the two variants in burnt, peeling skin}. I've also heard that shaving cream and black tea can do similar things…but I don't normally travel with those.

Now that you're ready for a night on the town—head out to dinner {and don't forget to bring some cash for the penny slots and your "pants vodka" for when you're not playing penny slots}. It should be dark now—or at least after direct sunlight—so the temperature will drop considerably {though still freaking hot}. You'll probably want to bring a light wrap for when you're in the casinos that can easily {and lightly} be carried when you're outside, plus if you're extra sun-kissed you don't want anything too heavy on your lobster shoulders.

There are a million options for dinner—you will find the perfect place that is appropriate for your level of food snobbiness.

──────────────── Again, Pro Tip ────────────────

Split dinner because you can't do anything with leftovers and there will be snacks later…if you're doing Vegas right.

Once you've finished dinner, just start walking! Walk through the casinos and see the beautiful architecture. Find the free shows the casinos put on {rain showers in the Miracle Mile Shops, dancing water at the Bellagio, Volcano at the Mirage, fire and water at Caesar's}. Look for fun gambling to do {again, the TV/movie based penny-slot games are my favorite—I'm probably gonna lose my money anyway, I might as well do it slowly and enjoy the show while I do}. Or, go shopping! Because you have your "pants vodka," you never have to worry about sobering up to the point of hangover or sleepiness...until you're ready.

And, with no open container laws you can even swing by one of the forty-seven CVS stores on the strip for a six-pack if that's more your speed. Grab a snack when you're hungry, some caffeine when you're fading...there is no agenda or time frame. When you're so tired you're not gonna be able to get your second {or third, or fourth} wind, head back to the room for bed time {and remember your cool, damp rag}.

Day 3–6: Just rinse and repeat Day Two with minimal changes to the evening activities. Maybe take a Lyft to Freemont Street for pizza at Pizza Rock and a fun time in "Old Vegas," maybe get tickets to a Cirque du Soleil show, maybe go to da club and dance the night away...so many options, so little time...

Day 7: Pack up, check out, take the midday flight home and sleep all the way there.

I know Vegas is not for everyone, I get that. {We can't be friends...but I get that.} Here's why I share my "ideal vacation" with you: it is just that—a true vacation. I'm out of my every-day element, so I don't have the pressures of day-to-day life {do the laundry, clean the kitchen, go to the store, make the bed} and also, it's a vacation, not a sight-seeing trip.

When you go somewhere new, you feel like you have to SEE ALL THE THINGS!!! I mean, who's gonna go to Paris and *not* see the Eiffel Tower, and the Louvre, and Arc de Triomphe, and Notre Dame, and Sacré-Cœur, and Champs-Élysées, and Musée d'Orsay, and Palace of Versailles, and Montmartre, and…if that's your vacation, you'll need a vacation after your vacation to recover from your vacation. While I do appreciate a good sight-seeing trip, sometimes you just need a "sit around, no time schedule, do nothing" vacation. And when you've been somewhere as many times as I have, that's what Vegas is to me.

Plus, Las Vegas is not "real life." There is no one on the strip trying to get to the grocery store or pick up their kids from daycare…literally everyone is there for a good time and to suspend their reality. I cannot think of another place on the planet that offers that {if you do, let me know…I wanna go}. All my vices are accepted and even encouraged in Las Vegas. Both my husband and I love to go, and we count down the days until we get to go back. Between frequent flier miles, hotel deals, and M-Life points, it's just about the cheapest vacation possible {even driving from Kansas City to Chicago and staying there is more expensive than a week in Sin City}.

Being out of my day-to-day element while still in my "element" allows my creativity to flow {in fact, the concept and mission of Sharing Solace was born in Vegas. Check out The

Sharing Solace Story on page 251 for more}. I am able to completely disconnect and just be. I'm familiar enough with my surroundings that I feel safe, and I don't have to be "on guard" all the time, and it rejuvenates me to go back to the "real world" and kill it {okay, maybe that's a poor choice of words}. I'm actually ready to get back on that plane and head home.

Maybe Vegas isn't for you…I can {almost} understand that {you just need to come with me sometime…}. I encourage you to find your version of "Vegas." Maybe it's a cabin in the woods, a shack by the ocean, a bench in the park, or your nose deep in your favorite book. Find THAT THING that removes and disconnects you from reality and allows you to wipe away all worries and cares…and go there as often as you can.

No, it will not get rid of your worries and problems. When you get back, they will still be there. However, you will have been able to reset your mind—giving you time to re-prioritize what's important in your world {sometimes a step back is what is needed to make you realize what's *not* important}, and hopefully give you some clarity.

Now it's your turn. You pick where you wanna go:

Vegas is MY definition of **Happiness**, but not the real definition I suppose. **Turn the page** to learn what happiness really is.

Think you don't deserve a vacation, and the chance to find happiness, for a little while? Turn to **page 165** and **Stop Suffer Shopping.**

Don't think you have the time for a vacation or some "me time?" Then turn to **page 185** for an alternative: **Write It Down and Work It Out, B!tch.**

If **The Sharing Solace Story** sent you here, then go back to **page 251.**

HAPPINESS

———

So, happiness has a formula. Did you know that? Some nerd in horn-rimmed glasses with a pocket protector took an emotion and turned it into an equation. {I use "nerd" in the most loving way possible—I married one, after all.} While this makes my accountant heart sing a little, it makes my grief brain take a double-take...

Here's the equation:

$$Happiness(t) = w_0 + w_1 \sum_{j=1}^{t} \gamma^{t-j} CR_j + w_2 \sum_{j=1}^{t} \gamma^{t-j} EV_j + w_3 \sum_{j=1}^{t} \gamma^{t-j} RPE_j$$

In short, happiness = reality - expectations. There you have it.

All you need to do is make sure your reality exceeds your expectations every. single. day. for the rest of your life. Easy peasy, right? So just set your expectations so low {like six-feet-under low} that reality will always surpass your expectations and you're good to go! Or, just have the most amazing Instagram-worthy experiences constantly; then you'll always be happy.

Yeah, okay. But can you *really* be happy all the time? If you're happy all the time, then doesn't it just begin to diminish its "power"? If you're always happy, do you then become a "happiness junkie" always looking for your next, more powerful fix? It brings to mind the C. Northcote Parkinson quote, "A luxury, once enjoyed, becomes a necessity."

Sometimes, expectations just have to overcome the reality. There must be highs and lows, ups and downs, ebbs and flows. Life can't always be a Barney Stinson Get Psyched Mix "All Rise, Baby"…there has to be rise and fall. Without the fall, how do you know the rise is worth rising for?

This basically mathematically proves you cannot be happy all the time. There have to be downs for you to recognize the ups. There have to be ebbs for you to appreciate the flows. As much as it super sucks to have to experience the sads—it's really the only way we can truly experience the happys.

Now it's your turn. You decide where to go next:

Let's go grocery shopping. **Turn the page** for **Grocery Bag Grief.**

Just because you can't always be happy, doesn't mean you should always be sad. Turn to **page 159** and stay out of the **Grief Ghetto.**

Does this story make you a little sad…or mad? Maybe it's time to **Go Duck Yourself.** Turn to **page 197.**

GROCERY BAG GRIEF

Some people like to say they're "in" grief. That implies that I chose this. You get IN to bed, the pool, a car, a relationship, trouble... If I can get IN to something, then I can just as easily get OUT of it {fling off the sheets, dry off, open the door, break up, say you're sorry}.

Others say it's like the eye of the storm, where slowly, over time, the intensity dies down until the storm is gone. That implies the "storm" will eventually be gone and just be a fleeting memory {or a really cool story}. Storms eventually completely pass; grief does not.

I think that grief is something you carry. You're given this thing you absolutely cannot put down and you have to decide the best way to get it to the finish line {the finish line being death}.

When you first "get it," you don't really know what it is or how to carry it. It's heavy, it's awkward, it's big, and {somehow} it freaking shape-shifts and wiggles like a squirmy toddler. You start by doing everything you can do just not to drop it. That's your sole focus.

You start by carrying it like you're bringing in the groceries from the car {that were sacked by the fourteen-year-old bagger boy who's crushing hard on the cashier} and you're only taking ONE D@MNED TRIP.

So, you have "bags" of the "essentials" up and down each arm and in between every finger. Essentials being: {in order of importance} Ho-Ho, Twinkies, brownies, marshmallows, chocolate milk, {candy, candy canes, candy corn, syrup,} eggs, bread, rice, cereal, peanut butter, flour... And, somehow you have the bread bag wrapped around your neck {God forbid anything happens and the bread gets smooshed!} and you are clinching at least one bag between your teeth. You walk a few steps; things shift so you counterbalance. Your pinkie finger, which is carrying the bag with the precious eggs, is about to break off from the weight...but you hold on with all your might.

You can *only* focus on getting to the kitchen without dropping anything:

Don't talk to me.
Don't bother me.
Don't breathe at me.
Don't even look at me.

Some of the essentials you're carrying can rebound if they get dropped. The marshmallows can take a beating. If the flour drops there will be a little puff of smoke, but it can be salvaged for the most part. The Ho-Hos taste the same even if they're a little roughed up. The container of chocolate milk can be knocked around a little bit, but don't spill it…then you'll cry.

Later on in your grief journey you continue to have the same groceries, but you realize before you leave the car you have about three times the number of bags you actually need—so you consolidate before you even leave the driveway. The bags are still heavy and awkward, but you feel like you have a little more control of them {and you don't have to use your pinkies, neck, and teeth this time—though you better watch out for that bread}. It's still not easy…but it's easy-*er*. Also, since you've been carrying groceries for a while now, you've gotten stronger: You've built up some biceps and thigh muscles and your core is as strong as an ox.

As you continue along your journey, the contents of your "grief" change and you learn how to carry it better. Your "grief contents" somehow shape-shift so it can be carried in an old-timey suitcase. {You know, the kind without the spinny wheels?} Once you get comfortable with the old-timey suit-case, you'll upgrade to a big ol' duffel bag that can be flung over your shoulder, then you'll graduate to a hiking backpack where you can clamp it around your waist and put most of the weight from the "essentials" on your hips and shoulders, until FINALLY you get to the little trolley on wheels you can pull around behind you. You still have to pull that little trolley around with you everywhere you go—but it's so much easier to get around with that than the grocery bags.

You will also learn to pack your "essentials" in the bag more effectively. While the actual poundage never really changes… you disperse the weight and pack the heaviest stuff toward the bottom. You learn to use the space you have as best you can {oh look! This thing fits inside this other thing and doesn't take up as much room...} and if you're really lucky, you'll occasionally have a friend who will help you carry it "beach cooler" style.

...Although that doesn't ever mean you won't have one of those "*Home Alone*—oh crap, we're late—just throw everything in the bag and we'll figure it out where it all goes on the way to the airport" moments...

I can almost guarantee at some point along your journey the handle on your old-timey suitcase will break, and before you can get it fixed, you'll have to carry it around in a bear hug...

...or go back to the grocery bags...

...or the zipper on your duffel will split...

...or you'll forget to snap the waist belt on your backpack...

...or the wheel on your trolley will start doing that wiggle, wiggle, waggle thing...

But you'll always figure out how to get your bag fixed {and the more it happens, the faster you become at fixing it}. You'll be able to keep moving forward.

So now, my friend, that is technically all there is. We are through. That's the end. Fin. This is all she wrote. But we all know that's not how grief really works. We don't just get to close the book on it and shelve it away for another time...so I think we need to keep going...

Wanna learn more about the Sharing Solace "Haute Message?" Turn to **page 251** to hear all about the importance, symbolism, and strength of **The Sharing Solace Story** as I hop up on my soapbox.

Maybe we need to **Just F'ing Breathe** (turn to **page 69**); this whole grief thing can feel overwhelming if you try to "bite off" too much.

Now might be a good time for a reminder of just how beautiful Switzerland is. Turn to **page 227** for **Hallo Aus Der Schweiz.**

Or, feel free to close the book and sit in contemplative thought for five to ten minutes...or hours...but I'm still gonna need that 5-star Amazon review {wink, wink}.

THE SHARING SOLACE STORY

———

The moment Madelyn died, I knew I needed to do *something* to honor her life, love, and legacy, but I just didn't know what that *something* was. The "go-tos" just didn't cut it in my mind:

- A 5k run didn't feel right. Personally, I only run for two reasons: toward ice cream and away from bears.
- A golf tournament was completely out of the question. The closest I've ever been to a course is driving the golf cart around the parking lot with an adult beverage in my hand, and Maddie sure had no connection to golf {I don't care how much money they can raise}.
- A foundation was a decent idea, but you don't just *form a foundation* to just form a foundation. The foundation had to DO something. It had to have a mission.

And, there was nothing I could "blame" Madelyn's death on {other than my own d@mned bad luck} to raise awareness and money for. I also felt like there were plenty "general" foundations out there devoted to baby and child loss. The world didn't need another one just to have another one. If I decided that was my path, my time and energy would be better spent helping the organizations that already existed. {Plus, experts say if you're forming a foundation to do something that's already being done by another organization then don't waste your time—just help the first one.}

For the first five years after Madelyn's death, I was in my "grief infancy" and just trying to sort through the infertility gambit. I didn't know which way was up. I couldn't take care of myself let alone try to help others.

I filed my idea away in my "for another day" file and went back to just surviving day to day...until...

THE BEGINNING

...June 2015, almost five years to the day, on our annual anniversary pilgrimage to Las Vegas (see page 231 for Hey Baby, Let's Go to Vegas! if you haven't already). At this point, even five years into my grief journey, I was still just going through many of the "normal" motions—like vacations—but my husband absolutely needed, and deserved, the break. Not only was he taking care of his "normal stuff" {job, house, physical and emotional health...} he was also taking care of me—like the toddler we {should but} didn't have.

I was surviving {from the outside some might even have said thriving} in a self-employed job, but again, I was going through the motions and most days doing the bare minimum to get by {while making it all look easy with a smile on my face and a song in my heart; it was f'ing exhausting pretending all the time}.

One evening while in Vegas, we were walking aimlessly from slot machine to slot machine giving them our pennies {as one does} when we realized we were both sleepy and sober; neither of which is okay at 10:00 p.m. in Vegas. Pants vodka in hand, we headed to the closest hotel gift shop for some caffeine.

Well, at the Bellagio gift shop you don't just get a month-old candy bar and a tepid soda. You're offered a large assortment of candy and Coke, intermixed between fine crystal dishes, diamond rings... and for some reason this time, a couple of {seemingly out of place} base metal necklaces with words hand-punched into them.

Next to these plain necklaces was a little placard that said something like "Wear this necklace. Embody the word. When you meet someone else that needs your word, pass it along. Then tell us about it."

To this day, I couldn't tell you what the necklaces looked like, who produced them, or why my eye was drawn to that little placard {and not any of the shiny, sparkly things in the shop}.

I read that little sign over and over. And something clicked. An idea clicked. A concept clicked. The concept of Sharing Solace hit me like a bolt of lightning. Or more accurately, like my Madelyn up there, watching down on me, saying "Okay, Mama, it's time. This is what we're gonna do now.'

——————————— Side Note ———————————

You see, around this same time I realized all the "stuff" I'd received at Madelyn's funeral (the baby blankets, teddy bears, figurines, plaques, poems, pictures, etc.)—the things that once brought me so much support and comfort—now just brought back the pain of losing her. I had to get that stuff out of my sight...and out of my mind. (To this day, it sits in the back of a closet in my house.)

I realized that's not what these {at one time very meaningful} gifts were intended to do, or where they were intended to spend the rest of eternity. But, what do you do with this stuff now? I couldn't give it away, it was personalized, and I couldn't throw it away. Even though it now brought me sorrow, it was still chock-full of meaning.

So, this necklace in front of me was meant to mean something to the person wearing it, and when it didn't hold that same meaning, you're *supposed* to pass it along.

Okay, that's all well and good. I mean, the concept of "paying it forward" has been around for a long time. {I've been a "pay for the car behind you at Starbucks" girl for as long as I could drive...}

Something felt so right, and yet so wrong about these necklaces on the mannequin. So, my brain instantly went to work. This was now a working vacation...

THE CONCEPT AND THE FEELING

My brain was reeling with ideas and questions:

- Wouldn't it be cool to see something about who gave it to you {and who gave it to them, and who gave it to them}?

- Then you could see who you gave it to, and they gave it to, and they gave it to too…
- So that means it would probably have to have some sort of tracking something-or-other on it…
- Well, if it's gonna be able to be tracked, you should be able to know about those people, and maybe send them a thank you? Or share stories? Or something?
- But, do people *really* wanna give away something that held {hopefully} so much meaning to them?

I GOT IT! Two pieces, one they keep and one they give away.

And I continued working, every waking moment for three years straight, to bring this mission to the world.

This concept seemed to solve all the fundamental problems I was currently facing in my life at that moment: Why are all these gifts now just tchotchkes {and why/when did that shift in my mind happen}? What do I do with these tchotchkes now? And, how was I going to meaningfully honor Miss Maddie?

I was so pulled toward this concept {at this point it didn't have a name, it didn't have a look, it didn't have anything… just a feeling and an idea} that basically overnight I shut the doors to my other business and worked exclusively on this.

I realized early on it didn't really matter about the "thing" itself. Yes, it had to be appealing, pretty, non-cumbersome, easy to carry with you and inviting…, but other than that, it didn't matter what shape it took. The meaning was GIVEN to it through the situation, the symbolism, and the relationship with who gave it to them.

There were a few things I did know:

- The piece needed to be small and light enough that it could be carried or worn every single day.
- Everything {and I mean *everything*} about the piece, and the concept as a whole, needed to be intentional and meaningful.
- It had to be priced in such a way that it presented as something nice {not just another piece of junk} but not SO nice that the current owner wouldn't be willing to pass {at least part of} it along.

THE NAME

After pages and pages of every "'touchy-feely' word" available {I've never used dictionary.com more in my life, except maybe when I wrote this book!}, lots of "market testing" {"Hey, what do you think of this?"}, and a stroke of genius from my good friend Nate—the name "Sharing Solace" was born.

Sharing implies community and, well—sharing. Solace implies support and comfort in a time of distress and sorrow. Yup! That's it! That's exactly what we're doing!! Support, comfort, and community during a time of distress.

THE PIECE

A necklace felt right for a few reasons: I anticipated a large majority of our community {at least initially} being women.

Women like necklaces. A necklace is with you always; unless you choose to take it off. If you're like me, any time you are nervous/need strength/feel uncomfortable/or just bored, you "clutch your pearls." {I do it constantly and am always nicely reminded that "I got this" when I feel my necklace.}

So, what's it going to look like? Dozens and dozens of "prototypes" came and went—made out of just about every kind of material too: designs on paper, designs OF paper, air-dry clay, baked sculpting clay, old metal I found in the garage…I think I even made a few versions out of food… I was constantly feeling my Monica from *Friends* trying to find the perfect design and combination.

I arrived on a two-piece "set" because {other than just feeling right} there are LOTS of symbolisms.

- Grief is super heavy at first, and at some point you have to *choose* to release that debilitating grief. But, you never truly get completely over your grief, you'll always carry a little bit with you.
- Even once you choose to release the debilitating grief and move forward with your life, you will always be missing a piece of yourself. However, just because you will always have a little hole you are *still* a whole person.

Even the metal used is intentional. It needed to be strong enough to be passed along for years and years {traditional gold and silver are much too soft}. It needed to have some weight to it, so it could be felt, but not so heavy it felt unbearable. It needed to be hypoallergenic, so anyone could wear it. Cost-effective, so people would feel comfortable passing part of it forward. It needed to be solid metal {not plated} and hold its shape, color, and sheen through all conditions, so when it was time to take it off, it would be because you were READY to take it off, not because it was time to shower or get in the pool.

In all my research, the only metal that could do everything I needed was medical grade stainless steel {316L, for those of you who know what that means}—that presented a whole new problem. I didn't even have a design for this thing yet, but I knew hardly anyone would manufacture 316L metal jewelry because of its strength and durability.

Hundreds {maybe even thousands} of hours of online research, trade show walking, phone calls, and emails; I found someone who would help me functionally design and be the liaison between me and one of the four factories in the world that will manufacture medical grade stainless steel.

THE DESIGN

Awesome!! But I still don't know what this thing is gonna look like. {Blargh!} As I know absolutely nothing about design {remember I'm a bean counter by education and basically a "used car salesman" by trade}. I start looking for jewelry designers {if they can design how the necklace will *look*, I'll figure out the rest later}... Dozens of meetings later I find my designer! She not only does beautiful work but she also "gets" what I'm trying to do and hopes to make it as special as I want it to be.

Small glitch: after several meetings with her, she has a "feeling." She informs me this is not a project for her to design.

This is something that Madelyn and I need to design as a mother daughter team. Wha, wha, WHAT!?!?!

I'm uber ticked off at her {and everyone else for that matter}… but after some deep breaths {and a couple adult beverages}, I realized she is absolutely right. I got a cheap sketchbook and got to doodling.

I tried being exact—with measurements, proportions, and everything else, I tried closing my eyes and just putting pencil to paper. I even just took stuff and threw it at the paper to see if there was some "motif" that inspired me…

Turns out one of the very first designs I drew {and just about threw away} was the winner…after weeks and weeks of "designing."

———————— Long Side Note ————————

This little story here is not one I tell a lot of people {you'll see why in a minute}, but I think it's worth sharing. It is just one example of how much divine intervention has played a role in the whole Sharing Solace story.

I'd been working on token designs for a while {by now I'd settled on the two-piece set design and hoped, at some point, to have several designs for the middle token, but now I just needed the first one…}. I set all my ideas aside for a few weeks to let it "bake" in my mind, and so I could come back and look at it with fresh eyes to see if anything struck me differently.

While things were "baking," I found a stash of papers from right after Madelyn's death: funeral and hospital bills, a few greeting cards that never made it into the "card box," some notes I'd written about things I wanted to remember…and a hand-drawn design of a tattoo I planned to get…

Looking at that tattoo design, immediately I felt a warm déjà vu feeling wash over my body. I went to my sketchbook and basically overlaid the tattoo design with one of the token designs. I knew, just KNEW right then and there that THIS was the first token design.

I stared at the design for hours once I realized it was basically the same design from years earlier…I felt like there was something else I wasn't seeing {and that bothered me}. Maybe it wasn't oriented correctly? Or flipped? What was it that was bothering me so much!?!?

I started twirling the page and chills—head to toe chills. THAT is what I wasn't seeing. THAT was what I needed. THAT was the sign that this {and only this} could be the design for the first token. What I designed—just the ups and downs and topsy-turvy roller coaster of grieving—was really a sign from my Madelyn.

You see, if you look closely, as you rotate the token clockwise ninety degrees…you can vaguely see {if you're really looking for it} an "M," "E," "W," "3" with each quarter turn. Don't see the symbolism? Madelyn Elizabeth Webster made us a family of 3. Madelyn {it had to be her, no one else was smart enough or creative enough to have pulled something like this off…especially me} designed the token with her initials in there—just so everyone knew she was the one in charge.

Once I put all those pieces together I let out a little scream—I just couldn't wrap my mind around it. I was overcome with emotions. That HAD to be the design! After months and months of work, frustration, and irritation, Maddie laid it all out right there for me.

If I had forced that designer to create the design, if I had hurried the process, if I had done just about anything even a little bit differently, this would not have come to fruition the way it did. Madelyn was working her magic! Madelyn is in charge.

Alright, so now I have a name, a {concept of a} product, and a hand-drawn design…you'd think we're just about done, right? Just get all the balls rolling and you'll be in business in like, a second. Yeah, I wish.

Things still missing {besides the actual product}: packaging (and shipping boxes), all the stuff that goes in that packaging, do I need any kind of warnings on anything? A logo, marketing stuff…and {oh yeah!} the most-crazy in-depth website I'd ever heard of…

THE WEBSITE

The website was {and continues to be} its own special beast. Yes, Kyle COULD have created the website, but even though our marriage withstood the death of our only child, it would NOT survive the creation of this website {luckily we were smart enough to realize that before we started}. So, how do I find a web developer that both has the technical know-how to create a super complex back-end website AND the heart and sensitivity to express the feeling of our mission in "1s" and "0s"? Let's just say I kissed a lot of frogs before I found my prince{ss} charming:

- One developer {in one of our first meetings} told me, "I don't get how people can be so sad. When I'm sad, I just stop being sad and be happy!" Yeah, that twenty-something "frat-bro" was told to pick a finger as I walked out the front door.
- One developer came prepared to our meeting with a few loose post-it notes and a dull sharpie marker and was only interested in talking about how awesome his company was, and how it would cost a minimum of $35,000 to do an "in-depth SWOT analysis" to confirm my "silly little idea was even viable." Thanksbutnothanks. I'll see myself out.
- My favorite was the old dude {easily a thousand years old} who would only meet me in coffee houses and call me "honey" or "sweetie." I ain't your sweetie, and you're gonna see my sour side, buddy, if you don't shape up.

I was about to give up all hope and just live under a rock for the rest of my life when I met "just a young programmer" who told me I had to meet his friend. His company *could* do the work, but I probably wouldn't get exactly what I wanted, and it would cost way more than what was in my budget {like ten+ times what I had}.

I was a little leery to meet this "works-out-of-her-living-room" mom…not because I didn't think she could do the work…but because I was afraid she (or anyone that was a sole proprietor) wouldn't have all the necessary technical skills to do the work, or the community to figure it out.

What if she didn't get the concept of what I wanted? What if she didn't have the technical skills? What if we couldn't get a working and pulled-together website with all the bells and whistles by Madelyn's birthday? What if, what if, what if…luckily, I liked the guy that suggested her, so what could one meeting hurt?

All of those concerns melted away within moments of sitting down. As a female, and a mom, she got the feeling that needed to go into the site. As a loss auntie, she understood the pain of losing a baby shortly after birth. She seemed to have answers to all my technical questions {and more importantly, KYLE'S technical questions} and there was an emergency plan—just in case something happened. We became fast friends, who just happened to be working on a project together. That project being the biggest project of my life.

Shortly after we signed on the dotted line {and I paid my *very large* deposit}, I wasn't able to get a hold of her for a couple days. SH!T! Every possible issue I was trying to hedge against by spending the cash and using a larger company, all the concerns that I had thrown out the window because I liked this lady, came flooding over me. Did I just make the biggest mistake of my life?? {...And I used to cut my own bangs... that were also permed...}

Come to find out, her very healthy, thirty-something brother {the father of her niece that died shortly after birth} caught the flu, developed sepsis, and died within twenty-four hours. As selfishly concerned as I was for my project, I was absolutely heartbroken for her. I scoured the internet for her brother's obituary, so I could see where the services would be held. I needed to be there—for me. And, very secondarily, to tell her that work was not important {I'd figure it out}.

Before her brother's services were even planned, her "temporary replacement" had scheduled our next meeting and sent me the updated user flow. Looks like all my worries {hopefully} were misplaced.

It took a few weeks to get back on track, but she said Sharing Solace was the first project she came back to because of the meaning behind it, and that it even helped her, in its own special way, begin to heal. Now THAT'S what Sharing Solace is all about!

For the most part, everything else just started to fall into place: boxes were designed and ordered, pieces were shipped from Taiwan, marketing material was {painstakingly} printed...and all with only one lawsuit threat {further details cannot be discussed at this time}.

Over budget, over time, and over caffeinated, our website SharingSolace.com officially launched May 19, 2018—on my

Madelyn Elizabeth's would-be eighth birthday. This was my birthday gift to her.

─────────────── Side Note ───────────────

This book, the one you have in your hands right this second, is my would-be tenth birthday present to my darling daughter. Since I can't give her roller skates and ponies, she will just have to settle for her story, in written word, in the Library of Congress. Hopefully, she's not up there grumbling that it's not jellybeans and Barbie dolls.

THE WORK

Yeah, I guess if you look at it from a very, *very* high level, Sharing Solace sells necklaces to sad people. {And to be honest, if I can tell you're not open to the concept or have never had a devastating loss, I'll tell you that's what I do. It's just easier and will normally end the conversation and get you to walk away pretty quickly.} I had an old man once tell me (hand to God, his words—I promise) I was "going to hell for preying on the weak and vulnerable during their time of sorrow."

If that's truly what you see me doing over here, then I am VERY impressed you made it this far into the book. Give me a call, I'll help you find some friends—I have lots of enemies that would love to talk to you.

Sharing Solace, at its very essence, is a community of grievers for grievers. Our mission is to walk alongside you on your path toward your new normal. Think of us as your "Grief Sherpa": we help guide you when you need it, we help to carry the weight when it feels unbearable and give you encouragement when the terrain gets tough. We want you to know you do *not* have to feel alone, you are *not* crazy, and your thoughts and feelings *are* normal. Bigger picture: we know that even though not every day is a good day, there is good in every day.

We *just* happen to accomplish our mission in two ways: a technology-elevated, pass-along-able gift that is wrapped in a community of strength and support; and grief mentoring, programs and experiences to continue to build that community. {Again, come on over to SharingSolace.com to find out more.}

Now it's your turn. You decide how you'd like to move forward:

Just because I've learned to accept Madelyn's death doesn't mean it always feels good. Turn to **page 219** to see why **Grief Is a Broken Rib.**

Need a reminder that doubt and acceptance can go hand in hand? Turn to **page 205** for **When in Doubt, Get More Information.**

Or that acceptance and pain can coexist at the same moment in time? Turn to **page 193** for **Two Truths {and a Lie}.**

If you've been sent here from **Acceptance—My Personal Story**, head back to **page 211.**

BIBLIOGRAPHY

STAGES OF GRIEF

Kübler-Ross, MD, Elisabeth. *On Death & Dying: What the Dying Have to Teach Doctors, Nurses, Clergy, and Their Own Families.* New York: Scribner, 1969.

THE NEEDS OF THE MOURNING

Wolfelt PhD, Alan D. *The Journey Through Grief: The Six Needs of Mourning.* Center for Loss, 2016. https://www.centerforloss. com/2016/12/journey-grief-six-needs-mourning/.

Wolfelt, PhD, Alan D. *The Wilderness of Grief: Finding Your Way.* Center for Loss, 2007.

THIS MIGHT NOT BE YOUR TIME

Coelho, Paulo. *The Alchemist: A Fable About Following Your Dream.* Harper San Francisco, 1998.

KVETCHING SPHERE

Silk, Susan and Barry Goldman. "How Not to Say the Wrong Thing." *Los Angeles Times*, 2013.

https://www.latimes.com/opinion/op-ed/la-xpm-2013-apr-07-la-oe-0407-silk-ring-theory-20130407-story.html.

GRIEF GHETTO

"Bereaved Parents' Online Grief Communities: De-Tabooing Practices or Relation-Building Grief-Ghettos?" *Journal of Broadcasting & Electronic Media*, 2020. https://www.tandfonline.com/doi/abs/10.1080/08838151.2016.1273929?journalCode=hbem20.

Näppä, Ulla, Ann-Britt Lundgren, and Bertil Axelsson. 2016. "The Effect of Bereavement Groups on Grief, Anxiety, And Depression—A Controlled, Prospective Intervention Study." *BMC Palliative Care* 15 (1). doi:10.1186/s12904-016-0129-0. https://www.ncbi.nlm.nih.gov/pmc/articles/PMC4941031/.

GO DUCK YOURSELF

Hunt, Andrew and David Thomas. *The Pragmatic Programmer: From Journeyman to Master*, Addison Wesley Longman, Inc., 2000.

HALLO AUS DER SCHWEIZ

Kingsley, Emily. "Welcome to Holland." 1987. https://www.dsasc.ca/uploads/8/5/3/9/8539131/welcome_to_holland.pdf

ACKNOWLEDGMENTS

———

Wow, I never—in my wildest dreams—could have imagined I would be writing this. If you had told me ten years ago, or even one year ago, that I would be writing a book about my life with Madelyn, I would have laughed so much I pottied myself—I never could have believed I would be in a mental place to share.

They say it takes a village to raise a child. It also takes a village to memorialize a child. But, not just one child, this book is for all the sons, daughters, aunts, uncles, mommies, daddies, brothers, sisters, friends, and family that left this world before we were ready. This is OUR story; I'm just holding the pen this time.

I want to thank *everyone* who has come with me on this publishing journey {no matter how little they tell me they helped}!! I couldn't have done this without your interviews, feedback, advice, edits, ear to bend, shoulder to cry on, and support {physical, financial, and mental}. There are no words for how grateful I am.

A huge "Thank You" to my editors and publishing team for helping me trick everyone into thinking I "write good" and "look better." I promise, after I called you naughty words,

I calmed down and decided your constructive criticism was accurate.

I am very honored to be joined on this wild writing ride by some very special people. I would like to thank each individually {and allow them a few words of their own}:

- Carla and Sam Castrop, in memory of our granddaughter Maddie, my brothers, sister-in-law, and other family and friends that left us too soon. LYB
- Mimi Kathey and Papa Bob Webster, in loving memory of our precious granddaughter, Madelyn Elizabeth.
- The Dougan Family, in memory of our precious niece Madelyn Webster.
- Kevin, Lydia, and Bo Webster, in honor of our niece and cousin who will always be loved and never forgotten.
- Pam and Rick Heinz, in memory of our niece Madelyn Elizabeth and to support Crystal writing this book.
- Nan K. Holt, to support all the mothers and fathers of children who were lost much too early.
- Jeff and Carrie Behm, in memory of our son, Nick, and cousin, Madelyn. May this book bless many.
- Betsy Kirkwood Elder, for all families who have lost loved ones, especially those little angels who left way too soon.
- Elyse Noelle, in memory of my dad, Wes, and for all the people who suffer from a mental health disorder.
- Lissa and Jimmy Vogel, in memory of their sweet first daughter, Ava Faith.
- Monica Drake, in memory of our angel babies and in service to my doula families.
- Karen Camerato and Gerald Evans, in memory of Nicholas.

- Stephen & Deana Greengo, in memory of their only daughter, Harper Ruth. Too pure, too lovely, to live on Earth.
- Mallorie Isom, in memory of her angel twins, Simon Harold and Morris Emory.
- Lisa Sewalson, in loving memory of my mom, Barbara Morehead, and my dad, Marvin Morehead.
- Jennifer Palomino, in support of this great book that is going to help so many moms!
- Christi Schreffler, in remembrance of all who were called home, for they are dearly missed.
- Megan Payne, in support and love for the Webster family.
- Lindsay Nicholson, in support of one of my oldest and dearest friends!
- Abby Magariel, to honor those who grieve, and those who help others work through the grief.
- Jessica and Tuan Tran, for anyone who grieves the invisible or intangible. You are not alone.
- Cristi Hernandez, in loving memory of the tiniest angels.
- Lindsay M., to find peace among the broken pieces.
- Cathy Murphy, in support of those enduring unbearable loss. "Bear each other's burdens."
- Jan Smith, in memory of my precious boys, Ben and Zach, gone too soon.
- Brittney and Derek Prock, in memory of their son in heaven, Dex.
- Eric & Allison Koester, in memory of their family and friends taken too soon.
- Sarah J. Eaverson-Brinkley, in memory of Madelyn Elizabeth and in honor of Katherine Elizabeth. I like to think they would have been friends.

- Todd and Katie Harris, for all those who are and have fought cystic fibrosis and other incurable diseases.
- Christie Palmer, honoring the legacy of my love, Doug Blauer, who always helped those in need.
- Mendy Wright, in loving memory of my daughter Kaleigh Mundey. I will always see your light.
- Kevin and Lisa Truax, in memory of a precious baby girl and her very devoted parents.
- Dave and Rhonda Janssen, in support of a good cause and in memory of those we have lost.
- Mikie Lindemulder, in memory of her daughter Amanda Dawn. God Bless our Beautiful Children.
- Patty Adams Gustin, in loving memory of my Sonny Boy Khris and for his two sisters as he left us too soon.
- Brian and Lisa Bodenhausen, in memory of their son, Drew Bodenhausen. Your laughter and smiles are missed every day.
- Angela Hopkins, in memory of the one who made me a mom, Alexander, Forever 25. I love you, son.
- Stacy Dandridge Barnett, in memory of those I have loved and lost. See you on the other side…
- Ron and Jay Hicks, in loving memory of Kye Lyne and JoJo and in support of Crystal Webster.
- AshleyMarie, in memory of Jade Marie & Junior. It's because of you that I labor in love for others.

My love also goes out to: Stacey Mattson; Brian, Emily, Ava, Chloe, Fiona, and Damon Hooge; Jenni Zupfer; Amanda Wagner; Allison Stolte; Dorothy Nelson; Colleen McFarland; Tara Baikie; Marissa Vidler; Chel O'Reilly; Lauren Bristow Willams.

Continually updated grief resources can be found at:
SharingSolace.com/Resources

For Book Club talking points and additional
supplements please visit:
SharingSolace.com/BookClub

ABOUT THE AUTHOR

A true Midwestern girl, Crystal dips her fried food in ranch {mixed with a little ketchup for color}. Growing up in the heart of America taught her the world is what you choose to make it. You can have a great time at a root canal and a cr@ppy time at the Taj Mahal…if you allow yourself. Though her mentality has been tested time and time again – she's found a curious attitude and a touch of irreverence goes a long way in becoming truly resilient. Her quirky take on 'the suck' has awarded her opportunities to speak to national and international audiences alike.

Crystal's knowledge and personality are engaging and entertaining while stealthily adding in some 'book learnin'… for good measure. Popular demand for her unique approach led her to 'step up her game' with 1-on-1 and group grief mentoring. You can have a conversation with her too! **To schedule a complimentary discovery call with her please visit 'Work with Us' on SharingSolace.com**

When Crystal is not working – which, come on, she loves what she does, is rarely…you can find her aunting the sh!t outta her four nephews, binge-watching murders and musicals, enjoying all kindsa live entertainment, learning everything she can about the human mind, traveling as much as her pocketbook will allow, and consuming copious amounts of flavored vodka. She likes to stay well-rounded…

CPSIA information can be obtained
at www.ICGtesting.com
Printed in the USA
BVHW050835050323
659709BV00014B/943